THE PEOPLE'S
INSTRUMENT

THE PEOPLE'S INSTRUMENT

A Philosophy of Programming
For Public Television

By ROBERT J. BLAKELY

A Charles F. Kettering Foundation Report

Public Affairs Press, Washington, D. C.

To C. Scott Fletcher, who, if such things could be
measured, has probably done more than any other
person to bring public broadcasting
into being and set its course.

Published by Public Affairs Press
419 New Jersey Avenue, S.E., Washington, D. C.

Copyright, 1971, by Charles F. Kettering Foundation
Printed in the United States of America
Library of Congress Catalog Card No. 73-152564

INTRODUCTION

Television and radio have become inherent features of American life. No family lives in contemporary society beyond the light of the television tube or beyond the sound of the radio speaker. The forward march of technology promises a longer reach, a greater diversity and a wider program choice from these communications delivery systems. This ubiquitous technology can be a source of enrichment and enlightenment for Americans of all ages or it can fill the airwaves with a multiplication and amplification of mass appeal entertainment.

To enhance the opportunity for this enrichment and enlightenment, the public broadcasting system is being developed. From the reservation of television channels in 1952 has emerged a growing roster of television stations devoted to these broad educational goals. From the first experimental radio station launched on the University of Wisconsin campus in 1919 has come an expanding company of radio stations devoted to the same goals. For many years the supportive leadership of the Ford Foundation has assisted this progress through financial aid to individual stations and through the creation of national program resources.

The national consciousness was gradually awakened to the inherent value of this system for the public good. This consciousness prompted the establishment and the study and the report of the Carnegie Commission which, in turn, led to the passage of the Public Broadcasting Act of 1967. That measure gave public policy substance to the national development of a public broadcasting system committed to provide television and radio service in the public interest. It proclaimed the national objective of not only preserving but extending these technological resources for the benefit of the American people. To advance these causes the Act created a novel institution, the Corporation for Public Broadcasting, a nonprofit organization located between the public and private sectors. To perform this leadership role the Corporation would seek financial support not only from the federal government but from private sources as well. It would enunciate goals for the total system but not exercise control over the essential element, the individual stations. It would provide the financial means for the creation of national programs for transmission over an interconnected network of stations but it would not determine or produce those programs. It would serve as a spokesman for the total public broadcasting enterprise but would not own or operate any of its elements.

Early in the life of this novel institution it became apparent to its leaders that the great potential of public service must be expressed in the broad diversity and high quality of the programming offered. The program must be the message, the product, the service to the citizen customer. A broad range of programs was already available on the schedules of local stations. National Educational Television was offering to the stations a national program service covering areas of interest in public affairs and cultural matters.

But the new presence of the Corporation for Public Broadcasting and the new public mandate for the development of the system called for a re-examination of the underlying philosophy for programming goals. It was to that end that Norman Cousins, Winston Franklin of the Kettering Foundation, and I joined in organizing the Conference on Public Television Programming in June 1969 at the Wingspread Center at Racine, Wisconsin. The assembled experts, thinkers, broadcasters and administrators critically assessed the philosophical direction of this public enterprise. No past practice was spared in the critical assessments offered. No new idea was considered too innovative for thoughtful discussion. In the process of the discussion new creative alliances were formed among those who would apply the programming philosophy in the future. And out of those discussions came the thoughts and observations expressed by Robert Blakely in this volume. Mr. Blakely has captured the essence of public broadcasting's purpose and goals. He has set forth its historical background and endeavored to give direction to its future. He has truly specified "the people's instrument" for the future use of all Americans. He has demonstrated that the message must be the message if the great potential of these media for the improvement of the quality of American life is to be realized.

JOHN W. MACY, JR.

Washington, D.C.

PREFACE

Back in 1952 the Federal Communications Commission reserved for a year 242 television channels for possible non-commmercial use. What was to be done with those channels, the Commission explained, would depend upon whether educators and other community leaders could move fast enough to seize the fleeting opportunity. The Ford Foundation through its subsidiary the Fund for Adult Education was helping them move.

During that frenzied year I was Midwestern representative of the Fund, visiting many cities to discuss terms of grants-in-aid that the Fund was offering to universities, school systems, and not-yet-established community corporations. On a trip to Madison, Wisconsin, I talked with Henry Ewbank, then chairman of the University Radio Council. When I asked him about the width of the walls planned for the projected television studio, he laughed and said: "Oh, acoustics. Educational radio in the United States started on this campus. We solved the acoustical problem by nailing horse blankets over the windows. The main problem then was what to send over the air. It still is. The main problem of educational television remains the same."

Although at that time my role was to talk about facilities (which were, and still are, crucial), my real interest was in "what to send over the air." Therefore when, a few years ago, the Charles F. Kettering Foundation invited me, first, to attend its Conference on Public Television Programming, and then to write a book on "a philosophy of programming for public television," I jumped at the chance.

The Kettering Foundation gave me complete freedom in writing this book. Moreover, its staff consultant, Winston O. Franklin, helped me in many ways—with ideas, materials, "leads," ingress, etc. I thank the Foundation and Mr. Franklin in particular. But, just as my freedom was complete, so is my responsibility complete for the shortcomings of this book.

I would like to acknowledge my indebtedness to many other people also, but, once started, I would have to stop somewhere, and still some people would be unmentioned. Therefore, I will say that nobody was too busy to help me—in the stations, the Corporation for Public Broadcasting, National Educational Television, the National Instructional Television Center, the National Association of Educational Broadcasters, the Ford Foundation, the Federal Communications Commission and elsewhere. I thank them all.

To two men who wrote detailed criticisms of the next-to-the-last version of the manuscript I am grateful for pointing out errors, obscurities, lacks, and disproportions—Mr. James Fellows, Director of Professional Services, National Association of Educational Broadcasters, and Mr. David Davis, Program Officer, Office of Public Broadcasting, the Ford Foundation.

In laying the groundwork for this book, I made many visits and telephone calls. I attended many conferences. I wrote letters and received replies. I read and listened and watched. I remembered. But mostly I tried to think of public broadcasting as a whole—its history, its context, its relationships. Regarding broadcasting experiences in other countries, I decided to refer to them only to throw light on particular points in the American experience. After all, the broadcasting system of each nation, like its educational system, is its own kind.

The task was to discuss the *philosophy* of *programming* for *public television*. I have tried to keep that focus. But each of the three elements refused to be isolated.

Public television came out of public *radio*, and they are moving together into the larger field of public telecommunications. Moreover, *public* broadcasting in an important sense was made possible by *commercial* broadcasting: The American people have bought and buy sets to receive commercial broadcasting; equipment for transmitting, recording, control, etc., was developed from commercial broadcasting.

Programming, is, of course, the "payoff," the "product." But the product is the result of a *process,* and in public broadcasting that process is intimately related to many activities of people besides listening and viewing.

This book expresses a *philosophy* in the sense that I have tried to make a systematic statement of *basic principles and concepts in operation.* Principles, concepts and operations— all three run off into other aspects of American life.

In fact, Henry Ewbank's remark "The problem of public broadcasting is programming" is really a parable. The larger meaning was illuminated by Sir Geoffrey Vickers while writing on ecology as he looked out the window toward the great earth and stone circles of Avebury, England. There, four thousand years ago, human beings had dug a ditch twenty feet deep and a mile in circuit out of solid chalk and piled up an artificial hill three hundred feet high to protect their holy place.

"Avebury," Sir Geoffrey observed, "would not have been built unless the dreams of the decision-makers had taken that form and the total value system of the society had been sufficiently strong and stable enough to support the implications of that decision for decades. It was a strange dream for men who were little better equipped for digging than the foxes and badgers that shared their native hills. The lonely ring among the brooding hills reminds us that the quality of our dreams is neither masked nor redeemed by the quality of our technology."

The quality of our dreams is neither masked nor redeemed by the quality of our technology. The crudity of the picks of the men who dug at Avebury and the crudity of the levers of the men who raised at Stonehenge did not mask the high quality of their dreams. The "high fidelity," "high definition" and "living color" of broadcasting will not redeem the quality of our dreams if they are low.

That thought distills the justification for public broadcasting. It distills also the challenge to the people who direct and operate it and who cooperate with it. The purpose of public broadcasting is to enhance the quality of our dreams.

ROBERT J. BLAKELY

Chicago, Illinois

CONTENTS

THE NEED AND THE OPPORTUNITY

"We know what we are but we know not what we might be."
Mad Ophelia's words accurately describe the American people
as we now are. We know we are a democratic society that has
lost its sense of community. We know we are the world's most
powerful nation that has lost its sense of direction for the uses
of power. We know we are a people on the farthest frontiers
of science and technology who have not learned how to make
those forces serve humane purposes. But we do not know what
we might be if we recover a community of intentions, desires
and great common usefulness to ourselves and to other peoples.
We need new means for communicating and learning that will
enable us to understand ourselves and the world we live in,
and to work together for our common good. The American
people could develop broadcasting, particularly television, for
public purposes into an important instrument for becoming
what we might be.

This book is about that new instrument, which has no satisfactory name. At first it was called "non-commercial broadcasting," which says only that its purpose is not to make money.
Then it was called "educational broadcasting," which dissatisfies some people who think "education" has too narrow a meaning and dissatisfies some others who think it has discouraging
connotations. Recently the name "public broadcasting" has
come into currency, but there is disagreement on whether the
phrase includes instructional broadcasting. Although this book
uses all such names from time to time, it also uses the phrase
"broadcasting for public purposes" to suggest a conception
broader than the meanings of the other names. The best approach to that conception is, putting names aside, to review the
American people's needs and opportunities.

The most important needs and opportunities are those that

1

face all peoples. Generally these are problems that tend to get
the least attention because there is no adequate political or
social machinery for dealing with them. Yet if they are not suc-
cessfully dealt with—at first in smaller ways that support one
another and later in larger ways as suitable machinery is con-
structed—all partial efforts are bound to fail. Therefore, let's
begin by reviewing the needs and opportunities that the American people share with all other peoples.

Our Common Condition

The basic need is for human beings all over the earth to
realize that they are dependent one upon another, and all dependent upon the environment. In short, they must—or, at least,
should—use their power for the planetary good. The basic opportunity that the media of electronic communications provide
is to enable human beings all over the earth to become aware
of their interdependence and to acquire the knowledge and
skills necessary for cooperation.

Mankind has always despoiled his physical environment—
with fire and ax; with the grazing of domesticated animals and
the growing of crops; with hunting and mining; with dams,
canals and roads; with consuming and discarding; with hamlets,
villages, cities and ever larger cities. Until about two centuries
ago mankind was so few and puny that nature could absorb or
repair the damage. But now mankind is so numerous and powerful that much of the earth and many of its conditions are man-
made, not God-given. Nature, and therefore mankind, cannot
much longer endure the war that mankind wages against nature.

Groups of men have always fought one another. Until about
the last two centuries, they were so puny and so scattered
that, despite their local slaughtering, mankind could survive
and multiply. But now all human beings are so interdependent
and such powers of destruction are in hand that the species
cannot much longer endure man's war against man.

These two changes—in man's relation with nature and man's
relation with man—are both the unintended consequences of

science and technology, which vastly increased men's ability to alter their environment. Men used this ability for partial purposes. The larger world began to change in content, form and complexity at ever-increasing speed, far outstripping the growth of any corresponding power of control.

Massive forces are out of control. They and their consequences are compounding in two senses: They are increasing in the way that money increases when interest continually adds to principal; they are creating new totalities in the way that physical elements combine to form chemical compounds or in the way that parts combine to form machines.

Let us look at some of the major runaway forces, noting the compounding consequences and the final end that seems inevitable if they are not brought under control.

Compounding Consequences

The expected doubling of the world population in thirty years is only the arithmetical base, to be compounded by the rates of increases in industrialization. The indicated increase of 100 million American people by the year 2000 multiplied by even their present proportion of consumption and waste will be the equivalent of several billion more people.

The world is already running short of some materials indispensable to a technological society. Yet the drain on these and other resources will be compounded as the world population increases and industrialization advances.

The earth's ability to cleanse the wastes that are being released into its air, water and soil is already close to, if not beyond, the limit of its ability to sustain life.

There are weighty reasons to believe that several delicate balances on the planet essential to life as we know it are being tipped. Yet the imbalancing forces will be compounded as the population of the world increases and industrialization advances.

Some experts fear that as thermal, chemical and life cycles are disturbed, the deteriorating effects may snowball. All ecologists agree that, even without a swift, irreversible snow-balling, the continued accumulation of harmful alterations may sometime make the earth unable to sustain human life. That time may be only thirty or thirty-five years away according to some responsible scientists.

The earth could be made uninhabitable far sooner—any year, any day, in a few hours—by nuclear war. Both the United States and the Soviet Union clearly have no desire to use nuclear weapons, but the destructive capability of each nation continues to be multiplied. And every year more nations are acquiring the ability to wage nuclear war.

In 1969 an international research team headed by Gunnar Myrdal counted 120 armed conflicts between nations since the end of World War II. It estimated that total world expenditures for military purposes are greater today than the total world production in 1900 and that arms outlays are doubling every fifteen years, and, if continued, will by the year 2000 exceed the present total world production of goods and services.

The causes of war mount at least as fast as the expenditures for war. Consider the widening economic and technological distances between rich nations and poor nations, which are to a high degree separated also by race; nations severed in previous wars; the breakup of old colonial systems and the rise of new nations, many of which are artificial political constructions; competition for raw materials; overlapping "spheres of influence"; conflicting claims for territories and peoples; resentments of exploitations and restrictions; and everywhere the pressures of population and industrial production upon resources.

A review of the salient facts should note the increasing instability of political and social structures, both within regional blocs and within national societies. Since the 1950s both the Soviets and the United States have lost effective control over their "allies." Regardless of their forms of government, national societies, including that of the United States, are being strained by old and new tensions. These instabilities make it more difficult for national governments to deal with the great forces confronting them today.

Such trends point up the need for human beings all over the earth to realize their interdependence and to use their power for the planetary good. It's not enough merely to "repair damages" or to "repay a debt to the past." The task is to care for the health of the biosphere and to provide the stable conditions for enduring centuries. *Sometime man must* take conscious and deliberate responsibility for achieving and maintaining planetary balances. The difficulties increase with delay. The time when it is possible to do so is getting shorter every day.

Rebound or Transition

Clearly a stage of evolution is coming to an end. The stage when human beings, reckless of mutuality and the long-range future, could exploit nature and one another is approaching the barrier of endurance. The habituated response is to try to bulldoze through with greater power *over* nature and *over* human beings. But the barrier is absolute. The limit of human power over nature is the limit of nature's capacity to renew itself and to sustain life. The limit of power over human beings is the fact that the position of the many who have little to lose and are willing to die is superior to the position of the relatively few who have much to lose and want to live. An assault upon the barrier of endurance must inevitably rebound. It could rebound into the void—no future for man, perhaps no future for life on earth. Or an assault could rebound in a catastrophic throwback to primitive conditions. Then human beings would have to start their journey over again—a journey harder the next time because all easily accessible materials and fuels have been exhausted.

The alternative to the rebound—into the void or back to primitive conditions—is a transition into a new stage. It is the entrance into another dimension in which human beings use power *with* nature and *with* one another. To move into this new dimension requires that Man take a new view of himself and of life and act upon a new set of concepts. It involves changes in religious, moral, and aesthetic aspects of life just as much as it involves changes in what we know or hypothesize (science) and what we can do and decide to do with what we know (technology). It involves a concern for wholeness. It involves a concern for the long pull. It involves replacing the reckless drive for expansion with a prudent concern for enduring balances. It involves, in short replacing a concern for quantity with a concern for quality.

Which do we want—a rebound or a transition? The question cannot be ignored. Man cannot remain a malignancy, a kind of cancer, that destroys the larger living organization, and therefore itself too, by uncontrolled growth. Man must control and direct his own growth. His ability to do this lies in his ability to learn.

Two Worlds—Outer and Inner

"Man," "mankind" and "humanity" are useful shorthand terms. Psychologically, however, they are misleading. "Man" is conscious only in the awareness of individual human beings. Only individual human beings are able to learn. "The planet," "the biosphere" and the "environment" refer to realities, but this outer world is not the only reality. There is also the inner mental world where the real and the imaginary, the actual and the possible, the remembered past and the anticipated future all dwell together in the present experience of the individual human being. Only in his inner world does an individual human being learn.

This psychological fact leads us to a portentous question: How can we expect human beings, whose bodies and minds were formed by age-long selection in specific and immediate environments, to respond appropriately to an environment almost completely different? How can we expect that they will share enough common perceptions, meanings, values and purposes to cooperate for their common good?

To this portentous question a portentous answer is possible. Accompanying the need for human beings to learn a new order of responsibility is a new order of opportunity to meet the need. The developments that have set many forces in motion also give human beings new experiences, new conceptions, and new tools for controlling and guiding those forces. It is now necessary, and it is now also possible, for men and groups of men to think and feel comprehensively—in terms of wholes, the relationships of their parts, and long, intricate processes. It is now necessary, and it is now also possible, for men and groups of men systematically to define alternative ends and alternative means. It is now necessary, and it is also now possible, for the ideas and emotions of "mankind" and "the planet" to be, not vague abstractions, but personal concerns for ordinary people.

Science has deepened human beings' vision of the inter-connectedness of all things and thus has greatly enlarged the horizons of their thoughts, feelings and concerns. Science, of course, does not give meanings, values and ethics, but it provides larger and richer materials for new religious, philosophical, artistic and moral insights. Technology has made it necessary for human beings to be aware of the wider consequences of their decisions, and it has also enabled them to assume responsibilities over wider stretches of space and time. Science and technology together make it possible to expand the processes of decision-making.

The social neural system of these new capabilities is the new media of communications, particularly broadcasting. Radio and television enable ordinary people everywhere to be quickly, even instantaneously aware of occurrences throughout the planet and beyond. They enable ordinary human beings to perceive these occurrences with the vividness of primary experience. Indeed, the perception of events while they are taking place *is* primary experience—the experience of actual participation in the making of history.

Hundreds of millions of human beings have "been" on another planet and have "seen" earth whole—blue, small and lonely riding the infinite blackness. "That is our home!"—the root idea of ecology. "Earth is a spaceship!"—the root idea of

a closed environment that maintains its "life-support systems."
"If man can put men on the moon, man can solve problems on
earth!"—the root idea of the large-scale application of knowledge and power to solve large-scale problems. All over the
planet the ferment of these powerful simple ideas is working
to produce a culture in which common perceptions, meanings,
values and purposes may thrive.

Therefore, the basic opportunity is for human beings all
over the planet to develop the neural system of this new culture by using the media of communications to acquire the awareness of interdependence and to learn the skills of cooperation.

The Uses of Telecommunications

All nations have radio systems; most nations have television
systems; there are several regional radio and television systems.
During 1969 INTELSTAT, the consortium in which sixty-three
nations, including the United States, are represented, had four
satellites providing about 960 circuits in the Atlantic and Pacific
Ocean basins. A global satellite communications system is a
reality. But for what ends is this system to be used?

"Within each nation, and among nations, the wise use of telecommunications is a key to success in building and reinforcing the sense of community which is the foundation of social
peace: a sense of community based on freedom, and on tolerance
of diversity; a community which encourages and appreciates
the unpredictable richness of human imagination; but a community nonetheless, faithful to its own rules of civility and
order." Those words from the introductory chapter of the
1968 Report of the President's Task Force on Communications
Policy eloquently states the goal.

The governing word in that statement is the *wise* use. Telecommunications can be, and sometimes are, tools of tyranny.
They can be and sometimes are used to lie and distort, to
divide and confuse. The control of telecommunications is one
of the most fiercely guarded attributes of national sovereignty.
The American people can do little or nothing directly about

the uses or abuses that other peoples or governments make of
telecommunications. But whether the American people make
wise use of telecommunications is all-important to us and of
major importance to all other peoples.

Specific needs and opportunities for the American people in
the use of telecommunications is the main subject of this book.
The basic need and opportunity however, is for the American
people to use telecommunications to create a new sense of community.

A Program for the Future

"It is not yesterday, tradition, the past, which is the de-
cisive, the determining force of a nation. . . . Nations are made
and go on living by having a program for the future."[1]

The American people *have had* a program for the future. Indeed, the United States *has been* a program for the future.
"The American dream"—the infinite worth of each individual,
the individual as an end to which all things else are means,
equality of rights and opportunities, the sharing of freedom and
responsibility for the sake of individual development—these
traditional ideas are too familiar to need restating. In fact, they
no longer can be restated merely in words without an ironic
sense of the difference between dream and reality. Some groups,
rejecting the dream because they are unwilling to make it come
true for others, assert the right of "law and order." Some other
groups, rejecting the dream because they have become convinced that it will never come true for them, assert the right
of violence directed toward a "revolution." Still other groups,
finding no adequate meanings or values in American life, assert
the right of "anarchy."

But what binding force do the American people have —
except the belief that the American dream is a program for the
future and the intent to make it so? What idea is large and
flexible enough to provide all peoples with a program for the
future—except the idea of equal rights and opportunities for
all individuals? If the American people do not soon devise and

undertake a program for the future large enough to restore a sense of community, into what depths might we descend? Thucydides knew:

"Words changed their ordinary meanings and were construed in new senses. Reckless daring passed for the courage of a loyal partisan, far-sighted hesitation was the excuse of a coward, moderation was the pretext of the unmanly, the power to see all sides of a question was complete inability to act. . . . The moderates were destroyed by both parties, either because they declined to cooperate or because their survival was resented."

In America today, the "moderates" are those who cannot support law without justice, or revolution without program, or freedom without responsibility, or responsibility without freedom; who are aware both of the glacier of accumulated wrongs and of the lava of chaos just below the thin crust of civilization, and who have enough faith in the American people and the American dream to believe that a sense of community can be renewed.

These are the people, individually and together, who should take hold of the opportunity presented by the evolving system of broadcasting for public purpose and push it as far as it will go. How far this might be can be told only by exploration.

Broadcasting for public purposes is new, incomplete, malnourished and neglected. But it holds the seeds of larger things. Its potentialities will be discovered and developed only as large numbers and many groups of the American people come to regard it, not as an *institution,* but as *their instrument* to use for the purposes that matter most to them.

The need for the American people to develop the fullest potentialities of broadcasting for public purposes arises in part from the inherent limitations of commercial broadcasting in the United States, which the next chapter considers.

1. Jose Ortega y Gasset, *Invertebrate Spain,* Translation and Foreword by Mildred Adams (New York: W. W. Norton, 1937), p. 26.

II

THE LIMITATIONS OF
COMMERCIAL BROADCASTING

The wise use of telecommunications is a key to success in building and reinforcing the sense of community that is the foundation of social peace. In the United States the dominant use of broadcasting from the first has been, and still remains, in the hands of private enterprise for profit. The wise use of broadcasting to build and reinforce the sense of community in the United States and with other nations requires that the system of broadcasting for public purposes be developed into an adequate alternative and supplementary system of broadcasting: That need is the single argument of the review of commercial broadcasting made in this chapter. The aim is not to make a comprehensive report or judgment of performance. The aim is only to follow the thread of the argument from essential point to essential point.

The essential technical fact is that the frequencies for broadcasting are scarce. The essential political fact is that the frequencies in the United States belong to the people. The essential social fact is that broadcasting has profound powers to affect the people for good or for ill. The essential historical fact of broadcasting in the United States is that its present structure is largely the creation of private industries. The government of the United States has never even commissioned a study to devise and recommend the best possible structure for domestic broadcasting, as the governments of Great Britain, Canada, Australia, Italy, Sweden, Japan and many other nations have done. Because most Americans find it hard to think of other kinds of broadcasting systems or other uses or broadcasting than the ones they are familiar with, let us begin with another point of view—that of the 1960 British Committee on Broadcasting, chaired by Sir Harry Pilkington. [1]

11

The committee studied both radio and television in Great
Britain, but paid more attention to television. The British
have a dual system of public and commercial ("Independent")
television, with the Postmaster General over both, the British
Broadcasting Corporation in charge of public television, and
the Independent Television Authority in charge of commercial
television. The following quotations are intended, not to summarize the committee's conclusions, which were entirely restricted to Great Britain, but to give American readers another
vantage point from which to look at American commercial
television.

"By its nature, broadcasting must be in a constant and sensitive relationship with the moral condition of society. Broadcasters are, and must be, involved; this gives them a responsibility they cannot evade. (p. 15)

"It seems to us that 'to give the public what it wants' is a
misleading phrase: misleading because as commonly used it has
the appearance of an appeal to democratic principle but the
appearance is deceptive. It is in fact patronising and arrogant,
in that it claims to know what the public is, but defines it as
no more than the mass audience; and in that it claims to know
what it wants, but limits its choice to the average of experience.
In this sense we reject it utterly. If there is a sense in which
it should be used, it is this: what the public wants and what it
has the right to get is the freedom to choose from the widest
possible range of programme matter. Anything less than that
is deprivation.

"The alternative is often presented as this: that the broadcaster should 'give the public what he thinks is good for it.'
This philosophy, too, we reject as patronising and arrogant.
But it . . . is not the only alternative. . . . There is an
area of possibility between the two; and it is within this area
that the choice lies. The broadcasting authorities have certainly a duty to keep sensitively aware of the public's tastes
and attitudes as they now are and in all their variety; and to
care about them. But if they do more than that, this is not to
give the public 'what someone thinks is good for it.' It is to

respect the public's right to choose from the widest possible range of subject matter and so to enlarge worthwhile experience. Because, in principle, the possible range of subject matter is inexhaustible, all of it can never be presented, nor can the public know what the range is. So, the broadcaster must explore it, and choose from it first. This might be called 'giving a lead': but it is not the lead of the autocratic or arrogant. It is the proper exercise of responsibility by public authorities duly constituted as trustees for the public interest." (p. 117-18)

"Television has been called a mirror of society: but the metaphor, though striking, wholly misses the major issue of the responsibility of the . . . broadcasting authorities. For, if we consider the first aspect of this responsibility, what is the mirror to reflect? Is it to reflect the best or the worst in us? One cannot escape the question by saying that it must do both; one must ask then whether it is to present the best and the worst with complete indifference and without comment. And if the answer is that such passivity is unthinkable, that in showing the best and the worst television must show them for what they are, then an active choice has been made. This is not only to show the best in our society but to show also the worst so that it will be recognized for what it is. That this choice must be made emphasises the main flaw in the comparison. Television does not, and cannot, merely reflect the moral standards of society. It must affect them either by changing or by reinforcing them." (p. 19)

"Independent television is intended to serve two purposes. First, it is to provide a service of television broadcasting which will realize as fully as possible the purposes of broadcasting; that is, one which will use the medium with an acute awareness of its power to influence values and moral standards; will respect the public right to choose from amongst the widest possible range of subject matter, purposefully treated; will at the same time be aware of and care about public tastes and attitudes in all their variety; and will constantly be on the watch for and ready to try the new and unusual. Secondly, and inci-

dentally, independent television is to provide a service for
advertisers . . .

"The two purposes of independent television do not coincide.
Since the commercial product, the saleable product of the programming contractors is, not the programmes, but advertising
time, the commercial rewards will derive from making that
product as desirable as possible to those who want it, an aim
largely incompatible with the purposes of broadcasting." (p. 167)

". . . We conclude that, so long as this is so, no system of
specific controls by regulation will ensure the fullest possible
realisation of the purposes of broadcasting. To do this an
organic change of functions is required." (p. 169)

An "American" Philosophy Obscured

Does this philosophy of broadcasting sound "un-American?"
Actually, it is the philosophy guiding one of the main currents
of American history, obscured in American broadcasting by the
uncontrolled growth of commercial interests.

That philosophy is embodied in the First Amendment to the
Constitution, whose purpose, the courts have repeatedly held,
is to preserve an "uninhibited market place of ideas" and not
to permit "monopolization of that market," whether by the
government or by a private interest. In the Red Lion case,
decided in June 1969, the Supreme Court unanimously extended
that purpose to include broadcasting. For the Court Justice
Byron R. White wrote that the crucial right is the right of the
public to a multitude of ideas and experiences and this right
"may not constitutionally be abridged either by Congress or
the FCC."

That philosophy is embodied in the American people's massive
and varied support, public and private, of education, information and culture, going back to the 1787 command, "The means
of education shall forever be encouraged," continuing through
such legislation as the Land Grant College Act of 1862 and
still moving forward on thousands of fronts today.

That philosophy was expressed by the first annual National

Radio Conference called by Secretary of Commerce Herbert
Hoover in 1922, which urged that radio be regarded as a public utility and as such be regulated and controlled by the
federal government. In 1925 Secretary Hoover himself explained that by freedom in radio he meant the listener's freedom to hear and the broadcaster's freedom to meet public
needs.

However, the legislation that was finally passed and is in
effect today, for television as well as radio, diverted broadcasting in the United States away from public purposes into private
purposes. The 1927 Radio Act, changed little by the 1934 Communications Act, changed little by subsequent amendments,
provides essentially for a traffic control of transmission but not
for the enforcement of standards of service, diversity and
quality. Networks as such are under no control. Although
each station licensee must sign a statement that the frequency
channel is not and may not become a private property, and
although the license is reviewed every third year, the Federal
Communications Commission has rarely refused to renew a license because of poor station practices or programming performance.

The flaws in the ability of commercial broadcasting to serve
the public interest and in the ability of the FCC to enforce
standards of service and quality are both inherent.

The inherent flaw in the ability of commercial broadcasting
to serve the public interest adequately is that the broadcasters
make money by serving advertisers necessarily; make money
by serving the public only incidentally, if at all; often lose
money by serving the public well, and often can make more
money by serving the public ill.

The industry acknowledges the flaw. A key statement in a
study commissioned by the industry's trade association, the
National Association of Broadcasters, and submitted to the
President's Task Force on Communications Policy is: "the
commercial medium functions as a market instrument to move
goods and services for which someone . . . is willing to pay.

The limitations it must live with, therefore, are those of the market place." [2]

The limitations of the market place but a floor beneath which losses may not go and walls beyond which diversity of programming may not go, but they put no ceiling over profits and no floor beneath the quality of programming. How much money does the industry abstain from that could be earned through low advertising and programming? How much money actually earned is spent in raising quality and in diversifying programs? These are questions that the corporate ownership and management, accountable only to their stockholders, are free to answer.

They are not accountable to the broadcast industry. The National Association of Broadcasters has developed and administers codes of "self-regulation" both for radio and television. But many stations do not subscribe to the code, and many that do subscribe violate it at will.

Corporate ownership and management are not accountable to the Federal Communications Commission for the quality and diversity of their programming. Except in its ability to curb the crassest excesses the FCC is powerless. Its basic flaw is that it lacks independence—a flaw it shares with all other federal regulatory commissions.

"The commissions are dependent on the executive for appointments, for budget requests, and for political support; on the legislature for jurisdiction, for powers, for confirmation of appointments, and for appropriations. Lacking insulation from political pressures, they have been unable to take an independent line.

"More than this, the commissions have come increasingly to serve the interests of the industries they were set up to regulate. . . . Executives have made poor appointments and have failed to provide political backing. Legislatures have denied adequate jurisdiction, powers and appropriations. The commissions, lacking any other clientele, have turned to the regulated industry officials for support. They have become immersed in industry's problems and have come to share its point of view. The consumer interest has been lost from sight." [3]

What is the "consumer interest" in the case of broadcasting? The Communications Act of 1934 authorizes the Federal Communications Commission to grant a station license "if public convenience, interest or necessity will be served thereby," but does not define that condition. The FCC has rarely interpreted it in any way that has resulted in refusal to renew a license. No assessment of broadcasting performance has ever been made in the United States comparable to the British Report of the Committee on Broadcasting. Therefore it is necessary to examine the case that the industry makes for itself in its public relations and in presentations to the FCC, to Congressional committees and to executive agencies, such as the President's Task Force on Communications Policy.

This case can be summarized in four assertions: The industry serves the "public convenience, interest or necessity" well; alleged harmful effects of broadcasting have never been proved; the industry gives the public what it wants, and the broadcasting service is free to the recipient. Since the first assertion contains the terms that have never been defined, let us put it aside until we have examined the other three assertions.

The Effects of Broadcasting

Responding to the allegations of harmful effects from some advertising and programs, spokesmen for advertising and commercial broadcasting often say that the society would be what it is without the media, that the society shapes the media, and that their harmful effects have not been proved. It must be admitted that research gives little conclusive evidence of the effect of broadcasting upon values, attitudes, morality and behavior.

But, in the absence of conclusive evidence, presumptions must be made. What should those presumptions be? That broadcasting has no effect, for good or for ill? That to be real, an effect must be sudden, spectacular and isolatable? As in-

terested parties, advertisers and commercial broadcasters may
act upon those assumptions. As passive audiences, large numbers of the American people may acquiesce in programs and
advertising based on those assumptions. But in their other
roles and responsibilities—as parents and citizens, as persons
and publics—the American people must act upon the opposite
assumptions: that broadcasting is and will be a major force
in influencing the values and standards of our society; that
their influences cannot be clearly demonstrated precisely because they are pervasive, persistent and long-range; and that
some of these influences are harmful. If persistent, skillful
efforts to exploit human weaknesses do not have a long-range,
cumulative harmful effect, then the opposite must also be true—
that efforts to reinforce human strengths have no good effect—
and then all our attempts to develop better human beings and
a better society through the home, schools, churches and
community organizations are in vain.

The question of *purpose* is central. In broadcasting as a
branch of commerce, the purpose of the broadcaster is to sell
time, and the purpose of the advertiser is to sell goods and
services. They regard the listener-viewer as a *means* to manipulate to their ends. As a means they regard him in only one
role—as a potential purchaser. The many other roles that each
person plays in life, with differing responsibilities and behaviors,
shifting from moment to moment—as son or daughter, parent,
friend, worker, employer, employee, worshipper, learner, creator,
member of group or organization; as citizen of city, state, nation, world, — these roles are either ignored or appealed to
manipulatively. The home is a "market unit." The community
is a "local market." The nation is a "national market." The
unique individual of infinite worth, of unknown capacities and
fathomless complexity; the democratic society of human beings,
bearing the burdens of freedom to choose and of responsibility
for choices made—these are all summed up in one word:
audience.

And the commercial goal is the largest audience possible,
to increase to the utmost the value of the "time sold" by the

advertiser and the return from the "time bought" by the advertiser, to reduce to the utmost the "per-capita" cost of the program and commercial. Decisions about advertising and programming are made on the basis of "audience ratings." That these ratings are unreliable⁴ means that the decision-makers do not know how to do well what they are trying to do. What matters is that their objective is contrary to the public good. Decisions affecting the attention, perceptions, meanings, values and behavior of the whole society are made on the grounds of *quantity* at the very time when the major evaluational task facing the American people is to change from the uncritical pursuit of bigness to the critical quest for *quality*.

Decisions that subordinate quality subordinate the individual and the minority to the mass at the very time when individuality of person and group is already in danger of being overwhelmed by the mass. They strengthen the current toward mindless standardization instead of aiding in the creation of authentic identities and communities of diversity.

The commercial goal is an audience that responds to the imperatives of the advertiser; the democratic goal is a citizenry that responds to the imperatives of history. Insofar as broadcasting is only a branch of commerce, its influence is toward a passive mass that demands only to be diverted, while the social requirement is a people composed of active minorities that make demands upon themselves.

⋗ The outcome of the "numbers game" is programming that exploits, or lowers, the average tastes instead of trying to develop capacities—this when the need is for the excellent, the uncommon and the new. The outcome is programs that are trivial, or that are bland to please and timid to offend, or that ignore the questions most in need of being asked and evade the problems most in need of being solved.

Large numbers of the American people, particularly young people, are today either angry because they have been denied opportunity for affluence or disillusioned because they have experienced it. The dominant use of broadcasting to "push" and depict the affluent things and ways of the American society at this time is to feed the anger and to spread the disillusionment.

Most, if not all, of the standards by which the American people have lived are being at least questioned today. Insofar as programming, in the attempt merely to be "entertaining," depicts society as having already answered those questions by putting other standards, or none, in their place, to that extent is broadcasting destroying old standards and putting new ones, or none, in their place. Programs that portray sexual promiscuity, drunkenness, the use of drugs, corrupt business or political methods, disregard for the law and resort to violence as ordinary, even as attractive and rewarding, are programs that promote these kinds of behavior.

Such practices must be presumed to have harmful effects, and these practices implement the purpose of broadcasting as a branch of commerce, which is to attract and hold the largest possible audiences.

What Does the "Public" "Want?"

Another assertion by the broadcasting industry is that it "gives the people what they want." This contention was refuted by the British Committee on Broadcasting in words previously quoted: "It is in fact patronising and arrogant in that it claims to know what the public is, but defines it as no more than the mass audience; and in that it claims to know what it wants, but limits its choice to the average of experience. . . . What the public wants and has the right to get is the freedom to choose from the widest possible range of programme matter."

The most effective refutation, however, is in the fact that commercial broadcasting continually creates wants. In 1934 William S. Paley said that CBS would create an audience for classical music, and it did. More recently audiences for soap operas, quizzes, "games" and professional football were created in the same way. The cycle is familiar: first, a new formula that "clicks," then a rush to imitate, and finally a frantic haste to concoct new formulas as previously created tastes are jaded.

In cultural democracy, as in all kinds of democracy, the question is, How responsible and skillful are the leaders in converting needs into wants? Edgar Dale, who has been analyzing communications since the 1929-34 Payne Fund Research Studies on Theatrical Motion Pictures, drives to the heart of the question:

"... we need to talk more about needs and less about wants. To want something is not a safe standard for its value. Physicians know that, and distinguish between hunger (a real need for food) and appetite (which may be an artificial and learned habit). We may want food, but not need it. And we may need vitamins and minerals and fail to want them.

"George Washington gave us sound advice—good not only for those who want cultural democracy, but for those who think that helping people see and meet a need is more fruitful than always trying to give them what they want. Washington said: 'Let us raise a standard to which the wise and honest can repair.' " [5]

People who have the freedom and responsibility of governing themselves have certain bedrock needs, and leaders who try to help people meet those needs should not feel embarrassed by the charge that they are being "patronising and arrogant." One of the bedrock needs of democracy is for people to perceive reality with enough accuracy and to understand it with enough clarity to be able to make wise choices. Communications is a key factor in each of these three processes—getting the facts for clear perception, interpreting the meaning for clear understanding, and discussing for wise decision. The mass media, particularly television, are now the major instrument for public communication in the United States. Therefore, a central question is, How well do the mass media serve these three functions?

The first answer to that question must be that American commercial broadcasting confuses the very context of reality itself. To appreciate how deep and muddy the confusion is, we should try to look freshly at a situation that we have been conditioned to take for granted. Let us imagine that we are examining American commercial broadcasting for the first time through the eyes of an intelligent observer from another time or place—say, Candide.

Candide concentrates on television because it is the dominant medium. He learns that the numerous commercials are more than *parts* of the programming: They are the *reason* for most of the programs. "This program comes to you by the courtesy of . . ." "This program is made possible by . . ." The programs are the means to seize and hold attention for the commercials. "The sideshow is the show," he concludes, and therefore pays first attention to the commercials.

Candide observes that the line between advertiser and station is often blurred. Announcers of the purchaseable "we" are bought, along with the "time:" "Come! We will be glad to see you!" Similarly, the line between commercial and program sometimes disappears. Announcers and masters of ceremony, so familiar to the audience that they seem household members, endorse products and services as though they were disinterested parties. Some of these same announcers at other times present the supposedly disinterested news.

Candide notes that many commercials "sell," not just goods and services, but attitudes as well—usually mean attitudes toward what is desirable or worthwhile. One of the attitudes "sold" is that there are quick and easy answers to such personal problems as poor human relations, business failure and bad health, and to such social problems as insecurity and pollution.

Turning to the "entertainment" programs, Candide sees a few that are designed to help the viewer understand himself and other people better and to appreciate life more fully. But these are rare. Most of the programs aim only at diversion.

Turning to "reality" programs, Candide sees a few broadcasts that enable the viewer to share large historical experiences, immediately and at close range. But these too are rare. Reporting, interpretation and discussion play only a small part in the total programming, and most treatment is superficial, disordered and bland.

After viewing a range of different tyes of programs, Candide turns his attention to the "mix" of the types and parts. He watches during a representative period of "prime time." It opens with a short "roundup" of the news—first a filmed segment of actual combat, followed by a singing-cartoon commercial; then a simulation of a space mission, followed by a sexy commercial; finally a hop-skip-jump summary of news from Washington, Paris, Chicago and Cairo. After another commercial, the station management presents an editorial on the state constitution. Three more commercials precede a filmed drama about a "hired gun" in the "Old West." This drama is interrupted frequently by commercials, without regard to dramatic pauses.

Candide leaves the United States, despairing of discovering how the American people can even distinguish reality from fantasy, much less make such subtle distinctions as those between fact and probability, reporting and interpretation, disinterested analysis and self-serving advocacy.

The difficulties are deeper than any visitor from another time or place could possibly know. Science and techology are making the real world increasingly incredible. Public relations and advertising are making the false world increasingly plausible. The arts seem to be reflecting more and more of the chaos of society. More and more parts of society are taking on the contrived nature of art.

Commercial broadcasting compounds these confusions. It often exploits the looseness, brutality and chaos of the times, or merely reflects them without giving proportion or guidance. It sometimes permits itself to be exploited by others, from the promotion of shows to the "selling of Presidents." And at times it is hard to decide who is exploiting whom.

In sum, commercial broadcasting does not well serve the people's fundamental need to perceive reality accurately and understand it clearly. Its shortcomings are inherent: Its basic purpose is not to convert needs into wants—to inform, enlighten and educate—but primarily to cater to wants or create them in order to "sell time" by "delivering" large audiences.

The Costs of "Free" Broadcasting

Still another assertion by commercial broadcasting is that it is "free" to the recipient, in contrast, for example, to broadcasting for public purposes, whose costs must be borne by the public or by individuals and private groups. Because large-scale support will be required to make broadcasting for public purposes an adequate alternative and supplement, the assertion that commercial broadcasting is "free" should be examined at several levels.

On the surface, one cost to the consumers of "free" broadcasting is the purchase and maintenance of sets, which have been estimated to be more than twenty times the investment of the broadcasting industry; with such huge capital costs, set-owners deserve to have the widest possible range of choice of kinds of programming, not just a choice of turning on or off. Another cost to the consumer of "free" broadcasting is often higher prices for goods and services, and higher taxes to offset the advertisers' and broadcasters' business expenses.°

On a deeper level, a cost to the consumer of "free" broadcasting is the loss of the other things he might be doing. The cost of every expenditure of attention, time and life is the possibilities excluded because of the choice made.

On a still deeper level is the fact that every choice has a cost, which is one of the insights of ecology. The cost of attention and time consumed in passive diversion from problems is the consequence of the neglect of those problems. The cost of the uncontrolled growth of human population, of man-made resources and of wastes is the disappearance of unexpandable, irreplaceable clean air, clean water and empty space, and the lowering of the value, amenities and possibilities of life.

The cost of "free" broadcasting can be illustrated with commercial television for children. "Television and all who participate in it are jointly accountable to the American public for respect for the special needs of children:" So states the preamble of the Television Code of the National Association of Broadcasters. But on the screen, what are the "special needs of children"? To be treated as human beings, ends in their own right? To be protected in their helplessness? To be helped to grow in healthful ways? To be helped to distinguish between fantasy and reality? To be helped to see good and bad for what they are? To have programs that take into account the vast differences from developmental stage to stage? Wrong. Whoever gives these answers will win no prize. The "special needs of children" are toys, candies, cookies and cereals, sold by fatuous commercials, strung together with stupid cartoons that traffic in violence.

Although children may have such "special needs" served on some commercial stations on midafternoons and Saturday mornings, they can partake of the general fare with grownups in the early hours of the evening. Then they can see violence that is filmed or "live," as well as other "general entertainment." "Most of what we might think is rather pernicious passes over a child's head, but brutality does not: It hits it."[7]

Thanks not to the industry, but to public protests and to the example set by "Sesame Street" of the Children's Television Workshop, commercial television programming for children is beginning to change, with some concern shown for avoiding harmful effect, if not with any knowledge of how to achieve good effects. But the central question remains: Should children be regarded as means—as potential consumers? When a group of women from Boston proposed to network officials that children's programs be unsponsored, the officials, a member of the group reported, "kept coming back to the fact that we were asking them to give up revenue."[8]

Yes, the issue is always cost: lost opportunities to the advertisers; lost revenue to the networks and stations; cost to produce programs that are not obviously pernicious; tremendous cost to research, design, create, produce and present programs most likely to do good. Why should commercial television bear these costs?

But if harmful programs continue, the issue is still cost: harmful social effects. If innocuous programs or no programs are broadcast, the issue is still social cost: lost opportunity. If anything less than the best programs is broadcast, the issue is still social cost of lost opportunity. If the best programs are broadcast, the cost is money.

The choice is never between "free" and "cost." It is always between kinds of cost. The choice between the cost of harmful effect and lost opportunities, on the one hand, and money, on the other hand, extends far beyond programming for children. It includes programming for all the publics that make up the public, and for all the minorities that make up the American people.

Broadcasting as a branch of commerce does not have the purpose of serving the interests of these minorities and publics. A broadcasting service to the public financed by advertising does not have the leeway of profits or freedom to serve the interests of these minorities and publics.

To Serve the Public Interest

After examining three assertions by the broadcasting industry, the conclusions are: First, certain practices that must be presumed to have harmful social effects are inherent in broadcasting as a branch of commerce; second, whether the policy is "giving the audiences what they want" or "making audiences want what they get," commercial broadcasting does not adequately help the American people meet their needs for accurate perception, clear understanding and thoughtful deliberation; and, third, no broadcasting is "free," and the economics of commercial broadcasting do not support the kinds of programming designed to serve the special interests of the publics and minorities that make up the public and the people.

These conclusions throw enough light on the meaning of "public convenience, interest or necessity" to permit us to examine the first assertion made by the industry—that commercial broadcasting serves the public interest well.

Commercial networks and stations serve the public interest well in many ways. In the ways and to the degree that they do, they are paying the public for the privilege of making money by broadcasting on frequencies that belong to the public. But commercial broadcasting does not, and cannot, serve the public interest well enough. The needs are so great and of such kinds that an adequate system of broadcasting for public service is a necessary alternative and supplement.

The Prospects

If an adequate alternative and supplementary system is not developed, the prospects are that broadcasting will serve the public interest even less well in the future than in the past.

The economic vises on commercial broadcasting are tightening, with the sharpest grip on television, because it requires the largest audiences and has the highest costs. Ownership of sets has just about reached the ceiling. So has the time that most people can spend viewing television, and so has the percentage of people who can watch during "prime time." Television programming costs continue to rise faster than the general price level. Advertising seems to have about reached its level as a proportion of national economic activity.[9] Cigaret sponsors on TV must be replaced with other sponsors. Many advertisers are turning to other media that can "hit target audiences" more accurately. The television industry is hunting for new and a greater number of advertisers. The consequences are more and shorter commercials on both network and station programming, and a more frenzied drive to "deliver" large audiences and the advertisers' "messages."

Power in the broadcasting industry continues to concentrate. Power in the whole field of mass communications continues to concentrate. Power in the entire American economy continues to concentrate.[10] With such power in fewer and fewer hands, freedom to investigate, report, inform, interpret, criticize and advocate is proportionately constricted. Mass newspapers and magazines, and commercial radio and television stations and networks that have strong interlocking ownerships or interests are less likely to criticize one another's performance.[11] All the mass media are more likely to act with what is politely called "forbearance" toward the aggregates and conglomerates that own them, in whole or in part, or that dominate the fields of their interlocking interests and the total advertising budget.

This tightening coil of interdependence that concentrates power and restricts the freedom to criticize embraces the fields of politics and government as well. Politicians must raise money from corporations to pay the heavy costs of reaching the public through the mass media, particularly television. Corporations advertise in the mass media and often own them in varying degrees. Networks and stations cultivate favor with members of Congress to assure their licenses to broadcast. Members of Congress cultivate favor with the networks and stations to assure favorable treatment. A newspaper or magazine that has interlocking ownership with stations or networks has given a hostage to government. So has a newspaper that may benefit from legislation exempting it from antitrust legislation.

In these ways and others, the coil of mutual dependence of self-perpetuating power tightens in the United States—not the result of evil persons, or of "conspiracy," but the result, rather, of such vast impersonal forces as the growth and flexibility of the American capital market, the development of very large consumer markets since World War II, a continual rise in costs, the growth of systems analysis, and the large flow of engineers and scientists and scientifically trained managers into the American economy.

These forces do not work in only one direction. Struggles for power and its uses are fierce. Kinds of competition are multiplied and intensified in many fields, including that of the mass media. A kind of decentralization of decision-making within centralized control seems to be under way. The small stockholder is being wooed by management. Corporations are paying increasing attention to the motivations of their employees. But, in balance, the tightening coil of interdependence and power is making the American society less open—at a time when more and more individuals and groups are struggling desperately and often recklessly against the exclusions that deny them the right to participate in the decisions that affect them.

To return specifically to commercial broadcasting, the economic interests of the broadcasters have once again been reaffirmed as more important than the quality of their service to the public. During 1969, the FCC seemed to be moving toward a policy of making license renewal conditional upon evidence of more than minimal broadcasting performance. But early in 1970, under a Republican chairman and with a Republican majority in sight, the FCC adopted (or reaffirmed) a policy of renewing a broadcaster's license normally if he can show that during the preceeding three-year license period he has "substantially" met the programming needs of his community. What the FCC's standards for satisfactory performance will be can probably be forecast by remembering the commission has rarely refused to renew a license because of unsatisfactory programming and does not have the staff to make the necessary evaluations in about 2500 license renewals each year.

Backstopping the FCC as a protector of the industry's property rights is Congress. At any time Congress could enact legislation, such as the bill proposed in 1969 by Senator John S. Pastore of Rhode Island to prohibit the FCC from considering competing applications for a license unless it had first denied renewal of the existing license, which would effectively protect the broadcaster's "property" in his license. Ironically, Vice President Spiro Agnew's criticisms of broadcasting performance in the fall of 1969 strengthened the positions of the networks and stations. Many people whose main concern was to guard the freedom to broadcast against executive intimidation joined those whose main concern was to guard the broadcasting properties against loss of license for unsatisfactory performance.

A Conflict of Purposes

This review of commercial broadcasting has revealed it to

be a centaur. It is not a pure species of private business, like
an automobile manufacturing corporation, which can make a
profit by producing and selling a quality product. It is not
a pure species of a privately owned public utility, like a
telephone corporation, which can make a profit by providing
and charging for a quality service. It is not a pure species of a
public institution, like a library or a university, which is supported by the public to provide a public service. Instead, it
has two purposes—to make a private profit and to serve the
public interest—that coincide only rarely, usually diverge and
often conflict. The owners and managers of commercial broadcasting are held to strict private accountability for making a
profit and are held to almost no public accountability for serving the public interest. The conflict between the two purposes
is inherent and is more likely to intensify than to relax.

The men and women who must make decisions between the
teeth of these clashing purposes face a moral dilemma that
they cannot satisfactorily resolve. They deserve the understanding and sympathy of the American people because they too
are deeply involved in the conflict and the dilemma. As the
public, they want broadcasting to serve the public interest
well; as employees, as savers and investors, they want the
economy to grow. Tens of millions of them, either directly
through their own investments, or indirectly through their
pension and mutual funds, are stockholders in industries that
broadcast and advertise. As consumers of goods and services,
they are interested in some commercials and annoyed by others.
As citizens they want to know, understand and decide their
public affairs; as tired or bored human beings, they want to be
entertained and diverted. The decision-makers in commercial
broadcasting work where the sharp points of the moral dilemma
facing the whole society come together.

Fred Friendly, a major participant in some of commercial
television's finest public services, tells the story movingly in his
book *Due to Circumstances Beyond Our Control.* His title gives
the essence of the moral dilemma: The circumstances are beyond the control of any one person or any one group of per-

sons. He recounts an argument when he was President of the CBS News Division that he had with CBS Board Chairman William S. Paley and President Frank Stanton over the costs of unscheduled news programs. Friendly asked, "Mr. Paley, why do we have to make more money every year?" Paley responded, "That's a pretty good question, but we have many small shareholders across the country and within the company. Some of our employees have worked for us for a long time. Their entire security is tied up in their equity; many of them have stock options. Management's obligation is to protect the interest of those stockholders."

Friendly's account continues:

"Paley went on to expound the theory that if the management didn't maintain its growth and profits, it ran the risk of losing control of the company.

"Then the chairman of the board, who owns over a million and a half shares of CBS stock, was silent for a moment; looking at Stanton, he said, 'I suppose the mistake we made was in ever going public.' This was a reference to the stock capitalization of the company, which had previously been fully controlled by Paley and other top officers of CBS . . .

"That conversation provides a clue to the agony that plagues honorable men who must constantly try to balance the public good and private need. . . . The question is, What is enough profit? And conversely, What is enough public service? . . . Too many unscheduled news programs could drive [profits] down, could make Wall Street change its optimistic evaluation of CBS as a high-growth stock, could impel those mutual funds, foundations and universities to invest in something else." [12]

Insofar as the centaur of private broadcasting is a branch of commerce, it cannot reasonably be expected to do other than to serve commercial interests. Insofar as the centaur is a service to the public financed by advertising, it cannot reasonably be expected to meet all the broadcasting needs that the American people have. In either case, as things now are, the "circumstances" of commercial broadcasting are beyond the control of the American people.

1. *Report of the Committee on Broadcasting, 1960* (London: Her Majesty's Stationery Office, June 1962).

2. *Television and the Wired City*, by Herman W. Land Associates, Inc., prepared for the President's Task Force on Communications Policy, commissioned and published by The National Association of Broadcasters (Washington, D. C.: July 1968), p. 17.

3. Clair Wilcox, "Regulation," *International Encyclopedia of Social Sciences* (New York: Macmillan, 1968), Volume 13, p. 390.

4. Harvey J. Skornia, *Television and Society* (New York: McGraw-Hill and Company, 1965), pp. 127-136. He surgically reveals the unsoundness of the assumptions beneath the six major methods of collecting data used by more than 200 rating services, including the American Research Bureau, Bureau of Broadcast Measurement, Robert S. Conlan, S. D. Crossley, C. E. Hooper, A. C. Nielsen, Pulse, Elmo Roper, Schwerin, Sindlinger, David Starch, Trendex, and Videodex.

5. Edgar Dale, *Can You Give The Public What It Wants?* (New York: The World Encyclopedia and Cowles Education Corporation, 1967), p. 5.

6. See Skornia, *op. cit.*, Chapter V, "The Hidden Economics of Broadcasting" and his substantiating references.

7. Bishop Cockin, of the Church of England, *Report of the Committee on Broadcasting*, p. 30.

8. "Women's Group Urges Network To Take Ads Off Children's TV," by Fred Ferretti, *The New York Times*, January 7, 1970. The group of women, Action for Children's Television, in May 1970 filed with the Federal Communications Commission a survey of what it called "excessive commercialism on children's TV programs" and proposed that children's shows be sponsorless and perhaps made part of a station's public service requirement; that hosts of such programs be forbidden to sell products; and that children's programs for each station total two hours each day, or fourteen hours a week. The FCC accepted the group's proposal for consideration and received rebuttal from the National Association of Broadcasters and from individual television station owners.

9. For details on these four factors, see *Land, op. cit.*, Chapter III "Economic Factors in Diversity."

10. For a recent documentation of the concentration of power in the television industry, with much overlap into radio, newspapers and other fields, see "The Television Overlords," by Hyman H. Goldin, *Atlantic*, July, 1969, pp. 87-94.

For concentration of ownership in news media consult Hearings before the Subcommittee on Antitrust and Monopoly of he Committee on the Judiciary, United States Senate, 90th Congress, First and Second Sessions on S. 1312, "The Failing Newspaper Act," Part 5 (Washington, D. C.: U. S. Government Printing Office, 1968).

For a study of the concentration of business decision-making in "a very few corporations," see a staff study for the Federal Trade Commission, by Dr. Willard F. Mueller, submitted to the Senate Antitrust Subcommittee on November 4, 1969; this study noted that the 200 largest manufacturing corporations in 1968 controlled almost two thirds of all manufacturing industry assets—

a proportion of total assets that was equal to the share held by the 1000 largest corporations in 1941, even though the economy has grown enormously.

11. The unofficial organ of the broadcasting industry carried an editorial attacking the newspaper supplement *"This Week"* for an article "TV Violence" and a box "What You Can Do About It." The concluding paragraph of that editorial said: "If its performance was not up to broadcast journalism standards, *This Week* must be credited with exceptional bravery: Consider how the TV-station owners among the supplement's 40-plus newspaper clients must feel about disseminating in their own papers so one-sided an attack on a medium that, in so many U. S. communities, if not their own, is all that keeps the paper alive." See *Broadcasting*, July 14, 1969, p. 76.

12. Fred W. Friendly, *Due to Circumstances Beyond Our Control* (New York: Random House, 1967), pp. 183-4.

III

AN ALTERNATIVE AND
SUPPLEMENTARY SYSTEM

In the circumstances described in the previous chapter—-inherent limits to the public service that commercial broadcasting can provide and the requirements that the government can make upon it—a part of the answer is for the American people to support and take part in the development of an adequate system of broadcasting for public purposes. The development of such a system is not by any means the whole answer, but it is an important part of the answer. [1]

The development of an adequate system of broadcasting for public purposes is *within the control* of the American people. The system is even now a legal, physical, programming reality. It is incomplete and poorly financed, but it is healthy, ready to grow and capable of evolving. Public concern, public support and public use could quickly make it into a signifiicant alternative to commercial broadasting and an effective supplement to all other resources in public communication, including education. This chapter considers only the essential ideas of what an adequate alternative and supplementary system of broadcasting could be, leaving detailed discussion until later.

Ends and Means

For an adequate *alternative* to that part of commercial broadcasting that operates only to make a profit, the American people must be able to choose a significantly different kind of broadcasting. The ability merely to choose programs without commercials, or merely to choose more programs of the same kind, or even to choose a different kind of program will not be enough. No, an adequate alternative means a choice of a broadcasting that has a different *purpose,* that performs different *functions,* that pursues different *objectives* and that serves the American people as different *clienteles.*

The difference in purpose is defined in one of Immanuel Kant's imperatives: "So act as to treat humanity, whether in your own person or in that of another, in every case as an end, never only as a means." In the commercial system, the broadcaster and advertiser treat the listener-viewer as a means to their ends. Broadcasting for public purposes treats individual persons, publics and the society as ends in their own right, and itself as means to that end.

From that fundamental difference in purpose, there follows the fundamental difference in functions performed. Commercial broadcasting functions to form a mass that is passive except to receive and to purchase; broadcasting for public purposes functions to stimulate individuals and groups to be active in all their various roles, and to help them exercise their freedoms responsibly.

From these differences in purpose and functions, the fundamental difference in objectives follows. The objectives of commercial broadcasting are to get people to listen and view and to buy. The objectives of broadcasting for public purposes pertain to what happens in the lives of people as a result of the process of programming—the planning, the production, the presentation, the reception, and the consequences.

The purposes, functions and objectives of public broadcasting are different in kind, and therefore the clienteles it serves are different in kind. They are made up, mostly, of the same people who make up the audiences for commercial programs, but they are people acting in different roles, with different kinds of concerns, interests and reasons, just as the same person may concurrently read a mystery story for relaxation and a sociological report for understanding; just as he may attend a baseball game with ten thousand other fans one evening and a meeting of a voluntary organization with twenty or a hundred other members another evening. Broadcasting for public purposes may serve a large clientele at one time and a small clientele at another; it must serve a wide range of very different clienteles in any

one day or week. The members of these clienteles change and
shift from program to program, according to interests and
objectives. But they are always *publics,* and never a *mass.*

As Ortega has written, "... the most radical division that it
is possible to make of humanity is that which splits it into two
classes of creatures: those who make great demands on themselves, piling up difficulties and duties; and those who demand
nothing special of themselves, but for whom to live is to be
every moment what they already are, without imposing on
themselves any effort toward perfection, mere buoys that float
on the waves." [2]

Ortega's is an aristocratic faith. Broadcasting for public
purposes is a democratic instrument. According to the democratic faith, the distinction between the "mass" and the "select
minorities" is not so much a division within humanity as it is a
division within each personality. Most of us have a tendency to
float on the waves. Most of us have at least some tendency to
make efforts toward perfection. Commercial broadcasting exploits our tendency to be every moment what we already are.
Broadcasting for public purposes challenges our tendency to make
demands upon ourselves and provides opportunities to meet
those demands, individually and together.

Supplementary to What?

The role of broadcasting for public purposes as an alternative
to broadcasting for profit can be clearly defined by contrasting
principles. But the role of broadcasting for public purposes in
relation to the part of commercial broadcasting that serves the
public interest cannot be defined at all by contrasting principles,
because the relation is *supplementary.* The best one can do is
to try to ask the right questions and indicate at least the direction in which answers may be found.

Some of the questions are suggested by the dictionary definition of "supplement:" "Something added to complete a thing,
supply a deficiency, or reinforce or extend a whole."

Broadcasting for public purposes is the "something added."

But what is the "thing to be completed"? What would "completed" mean? What is the "deficiency to be supplied"? What is the "whole to be reinforced or extended"?

Should broadcasting for public purposes aim at being a supplement to the public service of commercial broadcasting? If the answer is yes, then it will always be responding to what commercial broadcasting does or does not do. It will never be more than an adjunct to the public service of commercial broadcasting. It will never enlarge the concept or improve the practice of public service beyond what is possible or permitted within the commercial framework. The commercial system, not the public system, will set the standards for public service. The influence of broadcasting for public purposes will more likely be to narrow, rather than to broaden, the public service of commercial broadcasting, and to relieve, rather than to increase, the pressures upon commercial broadcasting to remedy its own deficiencies.

Obviously, broadcasting for public purposes should aim to supplement something else.

That something else can only be the people's resources for public communication in the largest sense, including education. The public broadcasting system should aim at filling, not gaps in the commercial media, but gaps in people's lives. It should aim at supplying deficiencies, not in the commercial media, but in the processes of learning, and of social perception, understanding, interpretation and decision-making. It should aim at reinforcing the sense of community and extending the field of cooperation, and this "whole" will never be completed, for it includes the entire society and country, and, beyond, the entire human race and planet.

The conception of broadcasting for public purposes as a supplement to all the other resources for public communication in the largest sense raises bigger questions: What should its relations be with the other media of mass communication, commercial broadcasting, of course, but also newspapers, magazines, films and so on? What should be its relations with other institutions and agencies of public service, governmental and

non-governmental? These questions will be taken up in later
chapters, but one aspect of the relations between the public and
private systems of broadcasting must be considered here: How
can broadcasting for public purposes be an influence for improving commercial broadcasting?

While in certain ways the two systems are not competitive,
they are inevitably competitive in that they compete for the
time and attention of certain minorities of the American people,
and their performances *will be compared*. The effects of such
competition are not necessarily good.

The Committee on Broadcasting studied the effects of competition from independent (commercial) television, which was
introduced in 1954, upon the British Broadcasting Corporation,
which until then had had a monopoly on television broadcasting.
The Committee reported:

"What struck us . . . was first that the conviction that the
effect of competition had been either mixed, or wholly for the
worse, was widespread. Second, both classes of opinion were
largely at one in the belief that the range of subject matter
presented had not expanded to an extent commensurate with
the increase in the hours of broadcasting. The third thing which
struck us was this: that the criticism was not of competition,
but essentially of misapplied competition. Where it had not been
misapplied—in production technique generally, and in some
classes of programme—the result was generally regarded as
beneficial. But where the competition had not been for good
broadcasting realised through a successful and practical definition of balance and quality, the result had been for the worse.
. . . We consider . . . that the pressure of competition has sometimes caused the Corporation, consciously or unconsciously, to
depart in practice from its own ideal of public service." (Pp.
45-6).

Broadcasting for public purposes in the United States would
have a harmful effect if it relieved the pressures, from within
and without, upon commercial broadcasting to improve and
expand its public services and to raise the quality and extend
the range of its programming. "Misapplied competiton" with

commercial broadcasting would influence broadcasting for public purposes to set ceilings on its standards and put wall around its diversity.

The Influence of Freedom

How can broadcasting for public purposes compete, insofar as it must, with commercial broadcasting in such ways that the interacting influence will be beneficial to both? That, clearly, is one of the right questions.

The answer lies in the freedom of the public system of broadcasting, first, continually to experiment with, develop and demonstrate new types of programming and new ranges of services; second, to set such standards of excellence, diversity and service that a significant part of the American people will use them in appraising the performance of commercial broadcasting; and, third, to take the lead in the raising of tastes and the cultivation of publics that will attract commercial broadcasting to "move in." A large order; but the lists have already been entered, and the gage has already been thrown down.

Various changes are taking place that may help broadcasting for public purposes to meet the challenge. The educational levels of the American people are rising rapidly. Citizens are increasingly aware of problems and needs, dissatisfied with the present, and concerned about the future. Throughout the society, individuals and groups are demanding the right to be heard and to take part in the decisions that affect their lives. The Supreme Court has extended the people's right of free expression to cover broadcasting. A multitude of specific publics is evolving out of the undifferentiated public or "mass"—a trend that has already transformed commercial magazine publishing and commercial radio broadcasting, that is transforming commercial UHF television and may transform commercial VHF television.[2]

Of course, a division of the total potential audience into actual five- or ten-percent fractions could mean simply cutting the same audience into smaller segments, but it could, alternatively, mean the evolution of many specific publics out of the mass, as

it has done to some extent in magazine publishing, radio broadcasting and UHF telecasting. Here would be a prypoint for
public television to influence commercial television for the
better by cultivating tastes that would be marketably attractive
to commercial television. At the same time, a wide front of
developments in communication technology is vastly increasing
the diversity and flexibility of electronic transmission and reception. Such changes (which will be looked at more closely later)
are opening large opportunities for the public broadcasting system to define and play its own unique role and at the same time
to influence the quality of commercial broadcasting for the
better.

A Force in Its Own Right

Together, as an alternative to commercial broadcasting and
as an important new resource for public communication, broadcasting for public purposes is a significant force in its own
right.

The public broadcasting system should regard itself, and be
regarded, not as the "fourth network," but as the *first and only*
public network. A public station should regard itself and be
regarded, not as a second, or fourth, or sixth station in a community, but as the *first and only* station whose sole purpose is
to serve the public interest.

While the public broadcasting system is at once local, state,
regional and national, it is controlled in the local communities.
Each station is licensed and operates to serve the peculiar needs
and interests of its community. All the decisions to produce or
not to produce, to use or not to use resources from elsewhere—
world, nation or other stations, whether by direct interconnec-
tons or replaying—are made by the local stations in the light of
their managers' judgments of the value of the programs to their
community clienteles.

While the public broadcasting system uses the media of *mass*
communications, its purposes, functions and objectives are to
provide *publics* with a flexible, two-way instrument of com-

munication—from, by and with the people, not just to them.

The answer to the defects and shortcomings of the commercial system that today dominates broadcasting in the United States is not to replace it, but to provide alternatives and make it more nearly complete: to add, not to subtract. The answer to control concentrated in a few hands in the industry is not to transfer control to a few hands in government; it is to disperse control among the people. The objective is more, not less, freedom: a wider range of choice, more diversity of expression and reception, more and better services to more publics. Broadcasting for public purposes, to repeat, is not the whole answer, but it is an important part of the answer.

A Present Fact

The basic structure, all the essential parts and all the vital functions of a system of broadcasting for public purposes already exist in the United States, ready to be developed into an adequate alternative to commercial broadcasting and an adequate supplement in the whole range of communications.

That the basic structure, essential parts and vital functions of a system of broadcasting for public purposes exist in the United States, ready for development—that is a fact, for which the largest credit should be given to the policies and efforts of The Ford Foundation, both directly and through its subsidiaries. They gave the indispensable combination of leadership and funds and provided both direction and form to other leaderships and funds without which there would not be the system whose outlines will now be sketched.[4]

The Federal Communications Commission has reserved 656 television assignments for educational purposes according to a geographic plan (555 UHF and 101 VHF), and more assignments are being requested. The commission has reserved also a twenty-channel section of the FM band for educational pur-purposes.[5] Even added to the present AM and FM stations (some of which broadcast on non-reserved channels), this number of assignments is not enough for national coverage, but the FCC is working on a geographical assignment plan for educational radio similar to that in effect for educational television.

At the beginning of 1971 about 190 educational television stations were on the air, more than half of them on UHF channels; there were state networks in more than half of the states, with the number steadily growing, and six regional networks. The FCC has licensed educational channels to four types of bodies: school systems or school districts, state boards of education or similar state agencies, public state universities, and non-profit community corporations. The problem of getting money for these different types of stations differs according to the nature of their governing bodies. Although the first three categories of stations are primarily concerned with instructional broadcasting and the fourth is primarily concerned with broadcasting to the general public, all of the stations are engaged in general broadcasting and most of them are engaged in instructional broadcasting.

At the beginning of 1971 about 425 educational radio stations were broadcasting, 25 of them AM; there were several state networks and one regional network, in the Northeast (the Eastern Educational Radio Network). The number of state networks is increasing and a trend toward more regional networks is evident. The FCC has given educational radio licenses to colleges and universities, public school systems, independent schools, Biblical colleges, state councils, educational organizations, public libraries and municipalities. As with educational television, the financial-support problem of these radio stations differs according to the nature of their governing bodies. Educational radio broadcasting covers the spectrum of both instructional and general programming.

Beginning in 1962, Congress authorized matching grants for the construction or enlargement of educational television facilities. In 1967 this aid program was expanded to include educational radio facilities, and it has since been continued, although inadequately funded. The backlog of applications for these federal funds in both television and radio is large.

When the federal govemenment began to give assistance, first with funds for educational television facilities and later in other ways to both television and radio, it did so recognizing the federal funds were helping to build up a foundation already laid by the voluntary initiative of individuals, institutions and agencies at all levels of American life, and also that it was stimulating the continuing and expanding efforts of voluntary initiative.[6]

Several vigorous national agencies and arrangements now aid and give leadership to the public broadcasting system at all levels—local, state, regional and national. Chief among these agencies are the Corporation for Public Broadcasting and the National Association of Educational Broadcasters.

The CPB is a non-profit, non-governmental corporation established by Congress in 1967 "to facilitate the full development of educational broadcasting in which programs of high quality, obtained from various sources, will be made available to non-commercial educational television and radio stations . . ." The CPB's many responsibilities derive from that major purpose. These responsibilities include arranging for satisfactory interconnections between educational television and radio stations; maintaning contacts wth Congress, the FCC and the agencies of the executive branch of the federal government; securing and granting funds for programs to local, state, regional and national educational television and radio stations; marshaling and coordinating support for public broadcasting; fostering professional development; conducting or commissioning research; advancing promotion and public relations techniques; and stimulating the development of new program concepts, series and production capacities.

The National Association of Educational Broadcasters is a non-profit trade and professional association in educational television and radio, with both institutional and individual membershps. It provides services both to and for its members. Its activities include program and station services, information, professional assistance and research and development.

The CPB gets funds from sources other than the federal government. The NAEB receives grants for special projects in addition to its membership dues. The two agencies work closely together (in fact, the CPB was established as a result of the Report of the Carnegie Commission on Educational Television, which, in turn, was a result of a national conference convened by the NAEB). They both work closely with other agencies and institutions, both public and private, such as the Department of Health, Education and Welfare (which administers the facilities assistance program), the FCC and the Joint Council on Educational Technology.

The CPB and the NAEB, through their own activities and the activities of other agencies and institutions with which they cooperate, provide the leadership and the services that make national systems out of the local educational television and radio systems. For example:

Program Production and Acquisition. At the end of 1969 the two national centers for supplying diverse and high quality programs to local educational television stations were National Educational Television and Children's Television Workshop (the latter under the former administratively), both in New York City. Several major developments occurred during the first half of 1970.

National Educational Television and New York City's Channel 13 were consolidated. The new entity is the Educational Broadcasting Corporation, whose president has one executive aide concerned with television reportage of the New York metropolitan area and another concerned with the presentation of issues of national interest, including cultural attractions as well as news and public affairs. NET has been converted into the national division of the Educational Broadcasting Corporation where it retains and hopes to strengthen its function of being the major supplier of programs for nation-wide public television. Channel 13 (with a license from the FCC and also a charter from the State of New York) has petitioned the FCC to change its call letters from WNDT-TV to WNET-TV. In the consolidation, each division of the Educational Broadcasting Corporation remains semi-autonomous within its area of responsibility. The

Boards have been joined but there will be some double use of both staff and facilities. The Children's Television Workshop, whose main production so far has been "Sesame Street," has become an independent corporation.

Also in 1970 a new organization was formed to produce and distribute programs for the nation's public radio stations—National Public Radio, with headquarters in Washington, D.C., and basic support from the Corporation for Public Broadcasting. NPR provides "live" interconnections, both for immediate and delayed broadcast, of fast-moving daily programs in public and cultural affairs. NPR thus combines for radio functions that are divided in television between the National Division of the Educational Broadcasting Corporation (old NET), and the new Public Broadcasting Service (mentioned in the next paragraph).

Program Exchange: Interconnections. In 1969 the CPB began the permanent, regular interconnection of educational television stations that was mandated by the Public Broadcasting Act of 1967. Interconnections are managed by a new subsidiary corporation, Public Broadcasting Service, with a board made up of representatives of the stations, the CPB, and the Educational Broadcasting Corporation. Such national interconnections enable the system to broadcast programs simultaneously, some of which are "live" and immediately rebroadcast, others of which are previewed and recorded for later rebroadcasting. Public Broadcasting Service soon began so to schedule its network programming as to match its better programs with the relatively weak programs on commercial network, hoping thereby to compete advantageously on a selective basis. The CPB also has begun experiments with the National Aeronautics and Space Administration in the use of statellites to transmit television signals domestically. In 1969 the CPB began to work toward a comparable permanent, regular terrestrial interconnection of educational radio stations, which, organizationally, resulted in the formation of National Public Radio (described in the previous paragraph).

Program Exchange: Shipment. Educational television programs on videotape or film are available to local stations through NET Television, Inc. (a subsidiary of EBC) from Ann Arbor,

Michigan; Educational Television Stations/Program Service, Bloomington, Indiana; the National Instructional Television Center, Bloomington, Indiana; the Great Plains National Instructional Television Library, Lincoln, Nebraska; and Midwest Program on Airborne Television Instruction (MPATI), Purdue University. Comparable library and distribution centers for educational radio are the National Educational Radio Network (tape), now in Washington, D.C., and the Broadcasting Foundation of America, New York City, which gathers and distributes taped radio programs from and to nations throughout the world.

Assistance to Local Program Production. The CPB makes grants to local television and radio stations to produce or improve programs, most of which are distributed regionally or nationally.

Program Experimentation. The CPB helps support the National Center for Television Experiments at KQED, San Francisco, and the National Center for Audio Experimentation at WHA-TV, Madison, Wisconsin, and it has made grants to establish creative film centers at KLRN-TV, Austin, Texas, and WGBH-TV, Boston, Massachusetts.

Studies. Both educational television and educational radio are developing with the guidance of basic studies, which are being advanced through continuing analysis, research and planning. Educational television has the Report of the Carnegie Commission on Educational Television,[7] which was stimulated by a conference convened in December 1964 by the NAEB and the U.S. Office of Education. Educational Radio has the study of public radio conducted by Samuel C. O. Holt for the Corporation for Public Broadcasting and the Ford Foundation,[8] and an earlier study commissioned by the NAEB.[9] These two studies of radio were preceded by the conference "Educational Radio as a National Resource" at the Johnson Foundation's Wingspread Center, Racine, Wisconsin, in September 1966.

Moreover, these developments are taking place within larger social and technical developments that favor UHF television and FM radio, which are the bands used by most of the educational stations. Legislation passed in 1962 requires that all new television sets be capable of receiving UHF as well as VHF signals. Legislation is in sight that would require UHF tuning devices to be of quality equal to those of VHF. UHF commercial stations are steadily increasing in number and strength, thus providing a social context beneficial to educational UHF stations. While no legislation is yet imminent (although bills have been introduced) that would require all radio sets to be capable of receiving both FM and AM signals, FM commercial radio broadcasting and the sale of FM sets are both growing healthily, also giving a favorable social context to FM educational broadcasting.

Roadblocks

However, after all such affirmative accomplishments and developments have been cited, the conclusion nevertheless must be that broadcasting for public purposes faces formidable obstacles. In 1970 one quarter of the American people could not receive educational television stations because of geography, and another large percentage could not receive them because their sets were VHF only, or because the educational television stations were handicapped by low antennas, insufficient power or poor signals. Educational radio was at a far greater disadvantage. Although educational radio stations have been increasing by about two per month during the past several years, people in large areas of the United States do not have access to educational radio—either because there are no stations, or because many of the stations have power enough to reach only from two to five miles, or because the listeners' set cannot receive FM signals. Almost half of the educational radio stations have annual budgets of less than $20,000, and educational radio has no regular national interconnections yet.

The public broadcasting system at all levels is financed poorly, leaving little margin for program production, audience research, program promotion, the acquisition or improvement of equipment and other activities necessary for healthy growth. Although Congress has found "that it is in the public interest to encourage

the growth and development of non-commercial radio and television broadcasting, including the use of such media for instructional purposes," so far it has made only subsistence appropriations for this end. A long-range plan for financing the
public broadcasting system adequately has yet to be adopted.

Money and Imagination

The lack of money that is sufficient, dependable and free
enough to enable broadcasters to deal vigorously with vital matters is one of the main obstacles to the development of the public
broadcasting system. However, money alone will not be enough.
In addition to adequate money—indeed, in order to get adequate
money over a long period of time—the public broadcasting system needs to conceive its functions as vital to the American
people and to translate that conception into effective practice.

The potentalities of broadcasting for public purposes will be
realized only as it becomes, not an *institution* that tries to do
good things *for* and *to* the American people, but an *instrument
that the people use* to communicate with one another and to
learn what they need to know in the conduct of their essential
affairs, both private and public.

1. For many suggestions concerning other parts of the answer, see Nicholas
Johnson, *How to Talk Back to Your Television Set* (New York: Atlantic-
Little, Brown, 1970).

2. Jose Ortega y Gasset, *The Revolt of the Masses* (New York: W. W.
Norton & Company, Inc. 1932), p. 15.

3. "The historic fact of the division of radio audiences may also come to
pass for TV, where no program or station in any market will be able to deliver much more than 5 to 10 per cent of the viewing audience except for
unusual special events." — Edward M. Stern, vice president of Foote, Cone
& Belding, quoted in "TV Habit Changes May Help Magazines," Chicago
Sun-Times, January 12, 1970.

4. Although the purpose of this book is to express a philosophy of programming for public television, not to write a history, the role that The
Ford Foundation has played should be noted because without it broadcasting
as "the people's instrument" would not be possible.

When The Ford Foundation entered the field of philanthropy on a large scale and in a systematic way in 1950, it saw television as a medium that could implement educational goals, both in formal instruction and in adult liberal education. Not only was there no non-commercial television in 1950; there was not even an allocation of channels for non-commercial use. Initially the Foundation worked on three parallel lines: (1) The improvement of commercial television programs—through the Radio/TV Workshop of the Foundation, principally "Omnibus." (2) The establishment of educational television stations and the development of programs of a general cultural and informational nature for those stations—through the Fund for Adult Education. (3) The use of television for teaching—through the Fund for the Advancement of Education.

In 1962 the Foundation made a thorough study of educational television, concluding that the nation needed an alternative television programming service to provide serious and continuous treatment of major national issues in a manner not possible in commercial stations. Therefore it made a series of annual $6,000,000 grants to the National Educational Television and Radio Center (NET).

By the middle of the 1960s it was apparent that no foundation, or combination of foundations, had the resources to provide the level, quality and quantity of non-commercial broadcasting services that the nation required. Therefore, in August 1966 the Foundation responded to an FCC Notice of Inquiry on the question of the establishment of a domestic communications satellite system. The principal points of its submission were that such a domestic satellite system should provide free service for the national delivery of non-commercial and instructional programs and, further, that such savings as it might provide for the commercial networks could be channeled into non-commercial television. In a second submission, the Foundation announced that it had appropriated $10,000,000 for an experiment to demonstrate what non-commercial television could achieve with adequate programming funds and nationwide interconnection. That appropriation resulted in the two-year Public Broadcast (PBL) experiment.

Also in 1966 the Carnegie Corporation of New York financed a Commission on Educational Television. Its report recommended a "well-financed and well-directed educational television system, substantially larger and far more pervasive and effective than that which now exists. . ." It urged Congress to establish a federally chartered non-profit, non-governmental corporation to be known as the Corporation for Public Television. While stressing the importance of having private funds available to the Corporation, it emphasized the need for major support from federal funds. Finally it recommended that the system be diversified and "that the Corporation support at least two national production centers" and that certain key public stations throughout the country contribute regularly to national programming.

Congress passed the Public Broadcasting Act in 1967 and the Corporation for Public Broadcasting was created early in 1968. During the period of the Commission's study and Congress' action, The Ford Foundation finding that the community-operated stations were in financial jeopardy instituted a program of matching grants to help them improve their local fund-raising and operations. In 1968 it established the Project for New Television Programming, providing grants to individual stations for program proposals submitted in a national competition. The most notable of a number of successful programs coming out of this project was "Newsroom," of WQED-TV in San Francisco.

Nationally, while the Foundation continued a high level of support for NET, the Public Broadcast Laboratory was established as a semi-autonomous unit of NET. The first nationally interconnected broadcast by public television was NET's presentation of President Johnson's State of the Union message, followed by detailed analysis, in 1967. That fall PBL became the first regularly interconnected public broadcasting program, seen on about 125 public stations.

PBL had a remarkable impact on both public and commercial television. The magazine format, which PBL used in its first year, has now become a regular feature on both NBC and CBS. The impact of having an interconnected network of public stations on Sunday evenings provided the catalytic action needed to make it possible for the Corporation for Public Broadcasting to negotiate with AT&T for five-nights-a-week interconnection for public stations under a reduced rate. That interconnection service was begun in December 1968.

From 1951 through 1969 The Ford Foundation made grants to public television exceeding $185,000,000. It continues to provide both leadership and funds in the deveopment of public broadcasting, radio as well as television, as "the people's instrument."

5. This section already accommodates about 400 existing educational stations and could accommodate more with judicious allocation.

6. For a detailed account of the first decade of non-commercial television, see John Walker Powell, *Channels of Learning: The Story of Educational Television* (Washington, D. C.: Public Affairs Press, 1962).

7. *Public Television, A Program for Action* (New York: A Bantam Book, Grosset & Dunlap, Inc., 1967).

8. See "Recommendations of the Public Radio Study," *Educational Broadcasting Review* (Washington, D. C., the National Association of Educational Broadcasters). Volume 3, Number 3, June 1969).

9. *The Hidden Medium: A Status Report on Educational Radio in the United States* (New York: Herman W. Land Associates, Inc., April 1967).

FROM QUANTITY TO QUALITY

The public broadcasting system must become essential to the American people if it is to evolve into an instrument capable of serving their many purposes, private and public. This means that public broadcasting must move from the peripheries of American life into its centers. It must make significant differences. It must have impact. It must enter the arenas, becoming visible, even vulnerable. It must play for the highest stakes, risking the loss of support of narrow interests to win the support of those who would promote the public interest.

To do these things public broadcasting must have financing that is adequate, that is assured over a period of years, and that is free enough and from various sources to enable it to undertake tasks highly charged with interests, issues and emotions—tasks that, in a word, are vital and therefore controversial. To do so, it must produce and broadcast programs that, cumulatively, are received by and significant to *most* of the American people. The temptation is to say *all* the American people, even though none of our institutions or instruments of education, enlightenment and participation have yet succeeded in effectively involving all the American people. The public broadcasting system can neither take comfort nor make excuses from that fact. It must systematically try cumulatively to reach and be significant for all the American people.

The problem of money and audiences may be regarded as another chicken-egg relationship. However, even though philosophers may debate whether the chicken or the egg came first, evolutionists are concerned with the *process* that resulted in chickens that lay eggs that hatch into chickens that lay eggs. At the present stage of its development, the system of public broadcasting needs to hold and execute a conception of *essential social function,* because the translation of that conception into practice is the only way by which the American people, at several levels and from many sources, both public and private, will give the system the financial and other kinds of assured support it requires.

The public broadcasting system has passed the point of no-return. Now it must "go for broke." Its names have changed from "noncommercial" to "educational" to "public" broadcasting. Its operations have grown from a handful of provisional local stations into a national system that aspires to be permanent, pervasive and influential. These changes must be accompanied by fully appropriate evolutions in philosophy and operations.

This chapter reviews some of the potentialities of the public broadcasting system, particularly television, in its present state of development; then it analyzes the nature of the partnership between the people and the public broadcasting system that must be established if its potentialities are to be realized.

The stress will be upon the public television system rather than radio, because television is the more powerful medium and is in a more advanced stage of development, although most, perhaps all, of the remarks will be applicable to radio also. However, before we examine television, it is worthwhile to make explicit why public radio is an integral part of the need and the opportunity to develop an adequate system of public broadcasting.

Radio for Public Purposes

Television is *not* replacing radio in the United States, as the automobile replaced the horse. In 1970 radio stations totaled more than 7500. Radio receiving-sets outnumbered the people. Studies indicate that more people tune in a radio some time during the week than turn on television.

Radio is more simple, economical and flexible than television, both for the broadcaster and for the person receiving. Program materials can be gathered anywhere, any time. Editing, storing and playing are uncomplicated. Private individuals, teachers, etc., can easily and cheaply record the programs they receive and play them back for other purposes. Radio programs can be received wherever one is, and listened to while doing other things, such as housework and driving a car. Blind people and others who cannot view TV can listen to radio.

Radio can do some things better than television, such as broadcasting music, non-dramatic literature, and talks and discussions in which the visual element is often distracting. Radio leaves more to the imagination. For example, when the School of the Air of the Wisconsin State Network moved its long-standing in-school radio series "Let's Draw" from radio to television, it was discovered, according to program director Karl Schmitt, "that the children tended to copy the television pictures we showed them as a part of the series. Their imaginations did not work as freely as they do in radio." The same series is now presented in "Radio-vision," which combines color film-strips when needed with in-school radio broadcasting.[1]

In this general setting, educational radio is experiencing a new growth. The 171 educational radio stations on the air in 1925 (almost a third of all stations operating then) had dropped to thirty-eight by 1937. But when FM broadcasting was authorized the next year, the trend was reversed. By 1970 425 educational radio stations were broadcasting—all of them FM except twenty-five (most of these licensed to land-grant universities).

The general social setting is favorable to the development of FM radio. In 1060 the ratio of FM radio stations to AM stations in the United States was one to six; in 1970 the ratio was more than one to two. The sale of sets that can receive FM is steadily climbing.

In addition to its higher fidelity of sound, FM radio has two technical advantages over AM radio that seem destined to have enormous consequences for the future: It is capable of broadcasting with subchannels, and it is compatible with the use of satellite relays and community antenna receiving systems for television. The first advantage, known as "multiplexing," enables one, two, three or more additional signals to ride "piggy-back" on the main channel transmission of an FM station. This capability offers, not only the possibility of additional aural channels to several special audiences simultaneously, but also a means to transmit data to computers, teletype print-out; hard-copy reproductions of charts, graphs and schematic diagrams; and even slow-scan television. The second advantage—the compatability of FM with satellite relays and community antenna receiving systems for television—offers the possibility of vastly expanding the range of choice that will be available through transmission by satellites and cables.

Historically, the public affairs services of educational radio have been distinguished by the wide range of domestic and international issues they cover, the depth and breadth of treatment, and the authoritativeness of the experts whose ideas and knowledge they disseminate. More recently, educational radio has been moving toward more emphasis on national and international subjects at the very time that commercial radio has been taking a noticeable and perhaps irreversible trend toward local concerns. Moreover, educational broadcasters are giving the lead in developing the possibilities of multiplexing and of cable and satellite transmission. For example, on behalf of educational broadcasting, the NAEB has recommended that twenty percent of channels on CATV systems be reserved for educational use.

Beyond such present trends is the fact that research and development into telecommunications and educational technology—what can be done best by various components, singly and in combinations—require a holistic, or "systems," approach to radio and television as well as to other media. The nation needs a coherent system of public broadcasting, just as it needs a coherent system of public transportation. In a coherent system of public transportation, airplanes, railroads, trucks, buses, limousines, automobiles, motorcycles, bicycles and walking would all have their proper roles, each used for what it can do best, all planned to achieve an effective whole, with components working smoothly together. The consequences of the nation's neglect of its railroad networks because of airplanes and private automobiles warn us that public radio should not suffer a comparable neglect because of the higher glamour of television.

Radio is an integral part of the system of broadcasting for public purposes. Public television and public radio can work in tandem. Advance in public television can "run interference" for public radio. Recognizing these facts, let us turn attention to the potentialities of the public television system.

The public television system serves in four main areas today—broadcasting for general audiences, for children, for instruction and for continuing education.[2]

In broadcasting to general audiences, television must seek to serve at least three objectives necessary for the survival and healthy growth of the American nation: to renew a sense of community, to renew the social contract, and to improve the people's internal environment.[3]

To Renew a Sense of Community

As a first step toward renewing a sense of community, it is necessary to renew the senses of the American community. The American have gradually developed an illness that resembles one of the symptoms of leprosy: The special nerve-endings have ceased sending impulses of sensation, including pain, and therefore the whole body social does not respond appropriately. Many parts of the society have experienced suffering and damage without other parts of the society even being aware that anything was wrong. This breakdown in the neural system of the society is probably the main reason why many of the suffering parts have concluded that they must use extreme measures to call attention to their plight—demonstrations, disorders and riots, and even retaliatory blows to hit other parts of the society "where it hurts."

The illness of the American society is approaching disintegration. Not only have parts of the society ceased to be aware of what other parts are feeling; they have even ceased to care, or to realize that they, too, are being damaged. This creeping dullness of sensation and concern is the result of many changes in our society—increasing diversification, specialization and isolation, etc.—but a major cause is the failure of communications. Since we are all dependent upon the media of mass communications for most of our information about, perception of and attitudes toward the rest of the vast, complex and impersonal world with which we do not have direct experience, a large part of the failure of communications is the failure of the media of mass communications, particularly television.

Therefore, one of the main objectives of the public television system in its broadcasting for general audiences must be to help the various parts of the community to understand the other parts and to understand all the parts as a whole—that is, as a community.

Such understanding must be not just intellectual but also imaginative and emotional. What are these other parts? Who are the people? What are they like? What are their problems and achievements? What are their histories and their aspirations? What are their joys, their fears and their sorrows? How do they live? What does it *feel* like to be members of those other parts of the community? How do they look at life and the world? How do they regard and what do they feel about the other parts and the society as a whole? In what ways are they different from us—whoever "we" may be? What conclusions does our society draw from these differences? In what ways are they the same as we are? What conclusions should we draw from these samenesses? What are the relationships, or lack of relationships, between those other parts of the community and our part? [4]

Questions such as these must be raised by television for general audiences, and answered as well as possible, again and again, with many approaches and from many vantage points. Programming that furthers this objective must be both accurate and sympathetic. To be so, it cannot be just *about* the several parts of the community; it must be *for* them and, often, *with* and *by* them. Public television for general audiences must, to the utmost of its capabilities, give all parts of the community, and all kinds of smaller communities, access to the most powerful of all the media of mass communications and, through it, to the larger community and its many parts.

Renewing The Social Contract

A kind of social contract between those who govern and those who are governed is necessary for a stable society, and most necessary for a society guided by democratic ideals and inheriting a democratic tradition. The social contract implies a workable degree of trust and cooperation between those who govern and those who are governed, and of compromise in all social relations. It implies that those who govern will listen respectfully to those who are governed and respond to fair and reasonable arguments, and it implies that those who are governed will respect the authority of the government and limit their protests to ways that do not wreck the society. In the United States today, this kind of social contract is being dissolved from both sides of the relationship.

The governments of the institutions of the American society are hardening, becoming less responsive to the people. Governments should be defined more broadly than the formal machinery of the state to include also all the institutions and arrangements to which governing authority has been delegated in our economic, professional, educational and other affairs. Unresponsive legislatures and executives, crowded and insensitive courts, inflexible bureaucracies of all kinds, regulatory boards that favor the interests they are intended to regulate, the tightening coil of self-serving interests between political and economic powers, the concentration of all kinds of power in fewer and fewer hands, social inequalities and injustices perpetuated by majorities against minorities—such a list only suggests the calcification that is in process.

Faced with institutions that do not respond reasonably and fairly on the basis of principle, more and more of the American people are using naked power to achieve the ends they consider justified. While technology has multiplied and magnified the coercive powers of government, the fragility and interdependence of our technological society have multiplied and magnified the negating powers of the people. Resort to naked power often succeels in gaining particular objectives, but, even though these objectives may be justifiable, the success of the method erodes authority, and, what is probably more damaging, erodes also respect for principles, legitimacy and orderly methods. Resort to naked power is divisive and corroding. Not only are the people and the government estranged, one from another, but also the people are set against one another. A society that increasingly relies upon naked power is moving toward a state of anarchy, which Hobbes described as "a war of each man against every other man."

A central cause of the disintegration of the American society is a growing mistrust of mass communications—disbelief in both the "messages" and the media. Those who govern and control are substituting public opinion, which they can fabricate at will, for the people's decisions. In Harry Skornia's fine sentence, ". . . instead of the consent of the governed, it appears that the governing of consent, the manufacturing of public opinion, prevails more and more."[5]

Therefore, another of the main objectives of the public television system in its general broadcasting is to provide the peole with a medium of communications that will help to strengthen the social contract—between those who govern and those who are governed, and between the various groups of the people. Television that renews the social compact must be both believable and accessible. It must provide information, context and interpretation that is dependable and fair. It must perform public services that help solve problems and resolve grievances. It must be a forum for open, free and honest debate. It must be an instrument by which the people can participate in the making of decisions and can cooperate in actions that they agree upon.

An effective public television system can both strengthen the role of voluntary initiative and help restore an affirmative relationship between the government and the people. The increase in population heightens human tensions. Greater mobility of people means fewer roots. Not knowing one's neighbors means not knowing one's self. But there is no alternative to the effort to renew the social compact. Indeed, as the nation moves toward the ordering of priorities and coherent efforts to solve large problems according to large designs, the need mounts for a wider sharing of values, meanings, objectives and trust. The public television system must seek to be a binding energy that will hold the American people together.

To Improve the People's Internal Environment

The usual phrases "cultural programming" or "cultural uplift" have connotations that are too limited—connotations of "high-grade entertainment" for a small well-educated, high-income elite, not of services essential to all the people. The third objective of public television for general audiences is stated in terms of the quality of people's internal environment because it is as important as the other objectives, to renew a sense of community and the social contract. Indeed, it serves these and other objectives.*

Cultural television, thus defined, must be broadly conceived, first in the role that the arts, including literature, play, or could play, in the lives of peole. The creation of art is the organizing of experience into meaning. It is self-discovery and the creation of identity, and at the same time an invitation to share and be shared. Art (always including literature) is the expression of personality and sensibility, the cultivation of what is most intimate, and at the same time an expression of what is universal. The artist is in some way an instrument for the spirit of his time, place and society, interpreting a world as it is experienced in a whole life. The artist is often the antennas of society sensing the future that will or ought to be before it is incorporated in practices or even words. All people to some degree are artists, and all artists are, first and last, human beings. Appreciation of the arts is in itself a creative

act. To appreciate art is to be open to experience, to welcome
novelty, to be intrigued by discovery, and to exercise capacities
for new imaginative thought and feeling. To appreciate the
artistic expressions of many lives, places and times is to enter
into many dimensions of our common humanity. Art, in a word,
is a kind of laser, which reorganizes the energy of ordinary
life and focuses it to achieve deep penetration and great range.
The arts, both in creation and in appreciation, can engage the
whole person in an unusual depth and intensity, with many
effects that are powerful and complex. Some of the arts can
pass through the barriers of words and languages, written or
spoken; they can penetrate differences of race and culture;
they can make all time—the past, the present and the en-
visioned future—a simultaneous now.

Cultural television must be broadly conceived as being significant to *all* the people. Art, through creation and appreciation,
can bring beauty, warmth and excellence to those people who
might otherwise never experience them, and it is most needed
by those whose surroundings are ugly and squalid. Cultural
television must give all who will view, or can be attracted to
view, a wider range of choice by widening their knowledge of
the range of choice. It must help rectify inequality of opportunity by giving all people a wide range of resources for enjoy-
ing the living arts.

Cultural television must be broadly conceived in time and
place, subject and media—respecting the here and now, not
just the there and then; drawing upon "pop" art, advertising,
posters, display, design of all kinds, tapes, films and photography,
science and mathematics and technology as creations of the
artistic spirit, as well as literature, drama, music, dance, paint-
ing, sculpturing and architecture.

Cultural television must take into account the broadening
universe of the arts—the amateur ("the lover") and the professional; the mixtures of media, the varying locales and agencies—poetry recited in bars and coffee houses, paintings on
sidewalks and walls, theater on little byways and above gro-
cery stores and in the streets and playgrounds, "Happenings"

wherever they may be, not just the arts in "centers," concert halls and museums.

Cultural television must take into account the many ends that the arts serve. Art, of course, is its own excuse for being, an end in itself. But the arts can also serve the ends of learning, of psychological health and of impetus to new values and behaviors. The telecasting of the arts is its own excuse for being. But it can also serve other ends: It can encourage the development of confidence and pride; it can help the different parts of the community understand one another better and to sense their commonalities. To break down ethnic and racial barriers, Julian Euell suggests the arts as "a connecting tissue with the outside society—motivating personal growth and development, and at the same time generating sympathy among divergent groups and individuals." [7] The arts should be an organic component, a pervasive spirit, in all the areas where television serves public purposes—broadcasting for general audiences, and also for children, the schools and continuing education.

A key to success in cultural television, as in television for social and political objectives, is open access and wide participation. Cultural television must provide, not just a means for audiences to experience and appreciate the arts, but a means for artists to express themselves and gain publics. It should be as concerned with the encouragement and development of artistic talent as it is with the opportunities of the viewers. Indeed, these two concerns are faces of the same coin.

Cultural television that is open and accessible is dangerous television. Art, by its nature, is a criticism of what is, a statement about what ought to be and could be. It is continually asking how the existing world can be altered to bring about a better vision of man and a better condition of life for all men. Art is a tool and often a weapon for bringing about changes in values, attitudes and institutions. Cultural television is dangerous because art is an explosive distillation of vitality. But danger is inherent in the evolution of the public television system into an instrument essential to the American people.

Television for public purposes in its cultural broadcasting for

general audiences has a responsibility to advance the ideas that
the arts are as organic a part of life as are science and technology, that our internal psychic environments are as important
as our physical external environments, and that the inner
visions of order, beauty and warmth that art gives us are
blueprints for a better world outside of us.

Television for Children

The public television system made a major breakthrough
during 1969 in the second main area of its service—broadcasting for children.

The ground was ready and the climate was right. The implications of research findings that the first four or five years of
a person's life may determine as much as half of certain
capabilities had begun to filter into popular consciousness. So
had the realization that the influence of television upon early
human growth may rival the influence of personal relationships
with parents and other children; most American children spend
three, four or more hours a day before the set, from infancy
through the formative years before they enter school and while
they are in elementary school. Alarmed by the spread of violence
and informed by such reports as those made by the National
Commission on the Causes and Prevention of Violence, the
American people took a fresh look at the exploitation of the
theme by the commercial media of communications, particularly in television programs for children. Many were appalled by
the standard fare that commercial television was feeding children. Citizens organizations, such as the National Citizens
Committee for Broadcasting and Action for Children's Television, gave leadership for changes and improvements.

In the favorable ground and climate, seeds of programming
for children had been planted and were being cultivated:
"Misteroger's Neighborhood" (produced and hosted by Fred M.
Rogers, who helped launch the country's first community-based
public television station, WQED-TV, Pittsburgh, and started
programming for children in 1954 with an initial budget of $30),

seen over many stations, with contributions from the local stations (and viewers, including children), the Sears Roebuck Foundation, NET and later the CPB; "The Friendly Giant"; "Kukla, Fran and Ollie"; "KaDiPus" of KDIN-TV, Des Moines (initiated in 1967 with funds from Title III of the Elementary and Secondary Education Act); "Volume C" (or "See"), also of KDIN-TV, with help from the Ford Foundation's Project for New Television Programming. But the breakthrough in 1969 was made by the Children's Television Workshop, with its "Sesame Street."

In 1966 the Carnegie Corporation asked Mrs. Joan Ganz Cooney to investigate the possibilities of preschool education by television. Following the report of her investigation, with the Carnegie Corporation and The Ford Foundation providing half of the funds and the U.S. Office of Education providing the other half, the project that became known as "Sesame Street" was started, and was under way when the Report of the Carneie Commission on Educational Television ranked broadcasting for children high in the responsibilities for public television, when Congress, in the Public Broadcasting Corporation Act, underlined the ranking, and when, in 1968, the new Corporation for Public Broadcasting decided to give priority to increased and improved programming for children.

The "Sesame Street" series broke through because it had the right combination of knowledge, talent and skill, made possible by enough money ($8,000,000) and enough time (two years— one for research and planning and one for testing, production, evaluation and presentation).

One of the premises of "Sesame Street," based on research findings, is that certain techniques highly successful in TV commercials can be used in learning. The series often has "commercials" that sell the value of learning and transmit the skills of learning how to count or how to recognize letters of the alphabet and the words they form. The program uses animation, fantasy and other methods effective in reaching youngsters. In its first year it was designed for all the nation's 12,000,000 children from three to five years old, and especially for children in disadvantaged neighborhoods.

Preliminary research indicated that youngsters who watched the series regularly showed "substantial increases" in letter recognition, and in logic, sorting, classification and enumeration. Responses to the program from children, parents, educators, critics and the general public were uniformly favorable. Surveys indicated that the program, broadcast by an estimated 200 stations, including some commercial stations, was reaching about 6,000,000 children, including large numbers of those in poor neighborhoods. These are large audiences for week-day mornings and afternoons and for Saturday mornings, measured by any standards. For example, in the Chicago area the program ranked first—with 32 percent of the viewing audience— at 9:30 a.m.

Let us not, however, start playing the "numbers game." The essential fact is not indications that millions of youngsters *viewed* "Sesame Street"; it is indications that those who viewed it regularly *learned* substantially. The significance of the large audiences is that large numbers of young children were enabled to learn.

"Sesame Street" was continuing beyond its two-year introduction, expanding opportunities also for children older than the three-to-five group it first aimed at; differentiating offerings for special minorities, such as children from Spanish-speaking homes; and raising its objectives to include more skills and understandings.

Other programs for children were in the mill of public television, particularly those produced and exchanged by local educational stations. For example, a consortium of twelve stations was at work developing programs using *Television Guidelines for Early Childhood Education*,[3] which was expertly designed to stimulate the thinking of television specialists and early childhood educators and to direct their efforts in improving television for young children. This booklet provides at least a preliminary map of the vast continent into which "Sesame Street" has broken through. It relates knowledge about the learning process, educational objectives, children and the medium. It outlines plans for particular learning objectives, themes, focuses and treatments, illustrating with specific ideas for programs.

The breakthrough that "Sesame Street" made illuminates the potentialities of television for public purposes in all the areas it serves. Testifying before the Subcommittee on Communications and Power of the U.S. House of Representatives in June 1969, the director of the Children's Television Workshop, Mrs. Joan Ganz Cooney, said: "Some of the architects of the public television industry have described the workshop as a prototype of what public television, and particularly the Corporation for Public Broadcasting, might be in years to come." She cited this expectation five months before the series began broadcasting. She was like Babe Ruth when he pointed to the right-field bleachers and then hit the next pitch there for a home run.

"Sesame Street" has shown what can be done through the "systems" approach to television and learning. It used scientific knowledge about the learning process. It put together the learner, educational objectives and the medium. It tested, modified ad evaluated. It was a model of the process of research, development and application.

"Sesame Street" illustrated what can be done with proper publicity and promotion, particularly in hard-to-reach areas, such as the ghettos.

It illustrated the possibilities of re-runs. Some stations broadcast the program twice in the same day. The series will be broadcast again. It will be a continuing national resource for years.

"Sesame Street" illustrated the potentialities of cooperation between the public television system and many individuals, institutions and agencies. For example, National Periodicals, publishers of *Batman* and *Superman* comic books, donated full-page advertisements and handbills recommending the program. The Columbia Broadcasting System radio and television stations aired hundreds of promotional spots. Both CBS and the Ameri-

can Broadcasting Company carried stories on their news programs. The Time-Life Broadcasting stations regularly promoted the series. Many newspapers covered the program—in
stories, with "plugs," and with favorable reviews. Department
stores and supermarkets distributed promotional literature. The
Urban League gave out literature at the Morgan State-Grambling
football game in Yankee Stadium. Among other organizations
that promoted the program were the National Council of Jewish
Women, the National Council of Negro Women, the National
Council of Churches and VISTA. The Radio Corporation of
America and other companies donated receiving sets to work-
shops and other educational centers. Public utilities and banks
included appeals for sets in their bills and payments; many newspapers published appeals for sets. The appeals were particularly
for sets that receive UHF because many educational stations
are UHF, and UHF set-ownership is low in poor neighborhoods.
The program was received in many nursery schools, day-care
centers, Headstart classrooms, and community and neighborhood centers. Youth Service Administration volunteers and
many others took part in door-to-door evaluation of the program.

"Sesame Street" illustrated that the public television system
can be a beneficial influence upon commercial television. Its
demonstration of possibilities was a major force moving all
three of the commercial networks to appoint vice-presidents in
charge of children's broadcasting and thoroughly to revise their
plans for such broadcasting.

"Sesame Street" illustrated ways by which educational television can be related to other media. For example, it became
the basis for a multi-media learning kit put out by Time-Life
Books (although it is expensive).

It has had innovatory influence upon day-care centers, nursery schools, pre-schools, kindergartens and early elementary
schools. It has been used in both pre-service and in-service
training of teachers. It has persuaded many parents that they
should and can use television to help their children learn, instead
of using the set as a handy but harmful baby-sitter.

Through its use in day-care centers and Headstart classes, "Sesame Street" has illustrated ways by which the public television system can be tied in with government programs and objectives.

"Sesame Street" has illustrated that learning can be enjoyable and that enjoyment can be educative. So doing, it has opened prospects to other possibilities for scientific, imaginative approaches to the education of older children and of adults, both in formal and informal learning. That is not to say that all "fun" is education or that all education can be "fun"; it is to say that some learning can be fun, that effective learning is entertaining in the sense of being interesting, and that all education should seek to be as interesting as possible.

Was "Sesame Street" costly? It spent $8,000,000 over a two-year period to research, plan, develop and produce 130 hours of programming that reached about 6,000,000 children the first year and enabled many of them to learn, that can be used over and over in this country, that can be used as it is in some other countries, and that can be used as a model in still other countries. This sum is low by comparison with the cost of NET programming during the same two-year period. It is even lower compared with the costs of commercial television programming. For example, $8,000,000 for *two years* is about half the sum that the commercial networks spent on a *single week* of evening-hour *entertainment* during the 1968-69 season.[9] However, although money costs and returns are important, social costs and returns are even more important.

A realistic *social* assessment would take into account also the alternative costs of continuing to squander, or even to damage, the nation's most valuable resource—its children—during their most formative years. A realistic social assessment would take into account also the fact that no means other than public television could achieve the desired results. Parents cannot do what "Sesame Street" did. Neither can nursery schools nor day-care centers nor pre-schools nor commercial television.[10] Only the public television system can achieve such results with children. A realistic social assessment would, therefore, regard the expenditures for educative children's television as an investment, not as a cost.

Television for Instruction [11]

In the third area where the public television system serves—instructional television—no breakthrough has been made comparable to that of television for children, which in 1969 opened up a new and empty land. Instead, at the beginning of the 1970s, instructional television held only a precarious beachhead in formal education, which is a vast continent of baffling jungles and formidable redoubts and which is governed by people with ancient and encrusted ways. Nevertheless, as the decade opened, encouraging preparations were under way for the systematic advancement of instructional television.

From the mid-1960s it was widely recognized that instructional television was not fulfilling the high hopes that many people had held for it. This recognition was summed up by Jack MacBride, general manager of the Nebraska ETV Network, one of the most effective of the state systems:

"If something happened tomorrow to wipe out all instructional TV, American schools and colleges would hardly know it was gone. I say this as an ardent, and undiscouraged, believer in the efficacy and importance and ultimate full use of TV in education. But TV is still far from the point of playing an integral role in education. We are still peripheral." [12]

Such judgments by knowledgeable persons do not detract from the honor due those broadcasters, educators and citizens who for nearly twenty years have struggled against great difficulties to realize the dramatic potential of television in instruction. Nor do they deny the substantial accomplishments in such places as the American Samoa, where the public school system was completely reconstructed to carry the core of the curriculum by television, or in Washington County, Maryland, where television is an integral part of the instructional program, linking forty-five schools by a closed-circuit system that can send six lessons simultaneously; or in Chicago, Illinois,

where the TV College of the City Junior College was used as a
model (both of what to do and what not to do) for the United
Kingdom's Open University. Nor do such appraisals doubt
the large body of research findings that students can learn
effectively from television.

On the contrary, such judgments affirm that there is no
alternative to continuing the effort to make instructional television an integral part of American education. Television for
public purposes needs to serve instruction more effectively because ITV is a major justification for the existence of the public
television system and a major part of its broadcasting; [18] because
many of the stations receive their basic support from local
school districts or state school agencies, and because much of
the backing in Congress for the public television system is given
with the expectation that it will be increasingly valuable for
instruction. Television for public purposes must serve instruction more effectively because it is a marriage of education and
communications and must seek to cultivate both partners together.

There are even more important reasons why instructional
television must become an integral part of American education. American education is in trouble because it is not more
productive, and the American society is in trouble because
education is not more effective. To increase productivity and
effectiveness, teaching will have to take advantage of technology, as other professions and occupations have done, and
instructional television is an important part of educational
technology.

Judgments that instructional television is now *in* but not yet
of American education reaffirm its potentialties when used in
concert with other resources, human and technical. It can make
education more productive and more individualized. It can
give education a more solid scientific base. It can make instruction more powerful. It can improve teaching. It can
make learning more immediate. It can make access to education more nearly equal.

Those knowledgeable persons who judge that instructional

television has not yet entered the center of American education are in remarkable agreement both as to the nature of the problem and the approach to its solution.[14] Their diagnoses and prescriptions were brought together and sharpened into recommendations for action by the Report of the Commission on Instructional Technology.[15]

The commission took as its starting point, not technology, but learning. "The heart of education is the student learning, and the value of any technology used in education must therefore be measured by its capacity to improve learning." It found that technology, properly supported and wisely employed, could help meet some of the nation's most pressing educational needs.

The commission defined instructional technology in two ways. In the narrow sense, it means "the media born of the communications revolution which can be used for instructional purposes alongside the teacher, textbook and blackboard . . . In nearly every case these media have entered education independently, and still operate more in isolation than in combination." In the broad sense, instructional technology is "more than the sum of its parts. It is a systematic way of designing, carrying out, and evaluating the total process of learning and teaching in terms of specific objectives, based on research in human learning and communication, and employing a combination of human and nonhuman resources to bring about more effective instruction." The commission made recommendations for an increase in investment in instructional technology in the narrow sense aimed at advancing the widespread acceptance and application of instructional technology in the broad sense.

The major recommendations were:

To establish National Institutes of Education within the Department of Health, Education and Welfare.

To establish within the National Institutes of Education a National Institute of Instructional Technology.

To establish in the National Institute of Instructional Technology a center or library of educational resources.

To develop projects to demonstrate the value of technology

for instruction initiated by the National Institute for Instructional Technology.

To support programs based on stepped-up research and development, to train and retain teachers, administrators, and a variety of specialists in order to improve the capacity of educators to make good use of technology.

To develop a mechanism whereby the National Institute for Instructional Technology brings education and industry together in a close working relationship to advance the effectiveness of instruction through technology.

Some of the commission's recommendations were embodied in President Nixon's Special Message to Congress on Education Reform, submitted March 3, 1970. He urged Congress to create a National Institute of Education within the Department of Health, Education and Welfare as a focus for educational research and experimentation. One of its goals would be "to increase the use of the television medium and other technological advances to stimulate the desire to learn and to help teach." The President also urged Congress to extend for three years the charter of the Corporation for Public Broadcasting, which, he said, would work jointly with the proposed National Institute of Education to "combine . . . modern technology and public policy to enhance our children's education."

It should be noted that radio is as integral a part of the new technology as is television, and the commission's study and recommendations, and the President's proposals include both media, in relationship with one another and in relationships with other tools, all aimed at the objective "to increase learning."

Thus, although instructional television has made no breakthrough, and although no breakthrough can reasonably be expected, a plan for steady, systematic advances is emerging, and agencies exist to help develop that plan. These agencies include the Corporation for Public Broadcasting, the National Association for Educational Broadcasters, the National Instructional Television Center, and the local broadcasting systems, both radio and television.

A World War II joke defined the difference between a Berliner and a Viennese. The Berliner says, "Things are bad but not hopeless." The Viennese says, "Things are hopeless but not bad." If one looks at what instructional television *is,* noting both a few successes and many obstacles, one can conclude, "Things are hopeless but not bad." If one looks at what instructional television is *not,* noting both the shortcomings and the opening prospects, one can conclude, "Things are bad but not hopeless."

Indeed, the prospects for instructional television are hopeful. The willingness to cooperate and the ability to stay for the long run are keys to success. The willingness to cooperate is a key because instructional television is only a part of educational technology, and educational technology is only a part of the fundamental reconstruction of American education that must be accomplished. The ability to stay is a key to success because the reconstruction of the highly institutionalized, widely decentralized system (or systems, or nonsystem) of American education will take a long time.

We are in only the early stages of a change in education comparable in significance to two earlier changes—first, when teaching left the family or the workplace and was put into the schools, and, second, when teachers shifted instruction from oral and handwritten methods alone to use also the printed page for instruction and self-instruction. Progress into the third era of change—when the new technology is harnessed to serve education—will have to be made undramatically and carefully, with many kinds of people learning together how to take a step at a time.

No "breakthrough" should be expected, because progress will have to be made against two continuing difficulties—the reluctance of institutions (their people and their practices) to try the new and unknown, and the mediocrity (or inferiority) of most of what has been done to date in the use of technology, particularly television, for instruction. The basis for such mediocrity (or worse) lies deeper than the lack of money: It lies in the false assumption that the goal is to find a more *economical* method of instructing. The results of successful use of instructional technology might well be greater economy, but the goal should be *more effective teaching* and *more productive use of human resources in education.* The Children's Television Workshop with "Sesame Street" had the right goals and made the right approach. It used research and experimentation; it learned from errors; it did not duck the problems of realistic costs—in research and planning, in testing, in the use of creative people, in production and in evaluation. Instructional technology, particularly television, will enter the mainstream of the instructional process from two banks, both of which are essential—by gaining acceptance with the educators, and by coming up with superior "products."

Television for Continuing Education

Continuing education—the fourth area where the public broadcasting system serves—is even less developed than the area of instructional television for schools and colleges.

Neither the Report of the Carnegie Commission on Educational Television nor the Public Broadcasting Act of 1967 was explicit about continuing education, but both implied its inclusion in their comprehensive statements of policy and objectives. The Public Broadcasting Corporation, therefore, was on sound grounds when it included broadcasting for continuing education as a major area of responsibility. Early in 1969 it commissioned the National Instructional Television Center, Bloomington, Indiana, to study and recommend how the corporation could best contribute to the field of adult, or continuing, education. [16]

The NITC review found that continuing education programming by educational television and radio stations was not unrelievedly bad. There was, for example, "Cancion de la Raza," produced by KCET-TV, Los Angeles, a large-scale mass communications attempt to reach Mexican-Americans by way of televised "educational soap operas," combining insights of the social sciences with the techniques of creative drama. There was the New Jersey Community Action Training Institute series "Ya Es Tiempo," produced by the poor for the poor. There was the video-taped "TV High School" produced by J. McFadden, Director, Manpower Education Institute of New York City, used by many educational TV stations for high-school-equivalency broadcasts. [17]

While the NITC review found that television and radio programming for continuing education was not *unrelievedly* bad, it was, in sum, depressingly bad. The programs were largely irrelevant to the urgent social needs of America, and their general approach to desired results was ineffective.

The depressing state of broadcasting for continuing education can not and need not be accepted as tolerable. Many urgent needs for continuing education will not be met if educational technology, including television and radio, is not used effectively. Many developments in educational technology, including television and radio, give reasons for realistic hope that at least some of these needs can be met.

The needs for continuing education should be seen in context. "The central social and economic role of land in a feudal society and of machinery in an industrial society is filled by organized knowledge in a science-based, noetic society." [18] Knowledge, or its lack, imbues all aspects of life and affects all relationships. In a dynamic society, effective knowledge is dynamic knowledge; learning must be continuous.

Let us focus on work, as a central example. In the United States today most work is based, not, as in the past, on skill gained through experience, but on knowledge—skills and information gained through education. President Nixon's proposed reform of the welfare program includes firm work requirements for eligibility and both opportunities and incentives for engaging in work-training.

The key to employability and advancement is knowledge. Let us note, then, that more than 56,000,000 Americans of eighteen years or older in 1968 had not completed high school. About half of them are potential students for adult basic education, and about half are potential students for high-school-equivalency education. Yet the pubblic schools are squeezed between rising costs and a taxpayers' revolt. How are the people who need basic and high-school-equivalency education to receive it if not through the imaginative use of the new technology, particularly television?

Poweiful forces are breaking down old concepts of education and opening the way for new concepts and practices of continuing education. The idea and practice are growing that education and work should be related from the upper elementary grades throughout life, sometimes together, as in work-study programs of various kinds; sometimes in alternating periods of years—with individuals moving into and out of formal education at many points in their lives.

But the traditional educational system does not lend itself to the flexible leaving and entering of formal education or to the shifting of careers in adult life. The field of continuing education offers an alternative to the constant lengthening of formal schooling into more and more years for more and more people. It offers a hope to alleviate, at least, some of the problems that attend that lengthening—the choices at earlier ages that lock persons into careers for the rest of their lives; the artificial prolongation of dependency for young people, with its consequent resentment and revolt, the rapid obsolescence of occupational skills, the artificial hastening of retirement from work.

"Extended schooling believes that the longer we keep the young away from work and life, the more they will have learned. Continuing education assumes, on the contrary, that the more experience in life and work people have, the more eager they will be to learn and the more capable they will be of learning." [19]

Continuing education is closer to becoming the "norm" of American society than most people realize. One 1969 estimate was that 30,000,000 Americans, with and without degrees, were engaged in systematic, planned instructional programs. [20] Another more sophisticated study estimated that in 1970 adults engaged in systematic education outside the conventional regi-

mens of schools and colleges numbered 60,300,000—a figure
slightly higher than the estimated number of students in 1970
enrolled in formal education, kindergarten through graduate
school.[21]

With such private and public needs for continuing education, the present "state of the arts" (if the phrase is appropriate) of television and radio programming for continuing education in the United States cannot be accepted.

Nor does it need to be accepted. The National Instructional
Television Center recommended that the Corporation for Public Broadcasting establish a national project for continuing public education broadcasting, using the "systems approach," and
making the materials readily available for extended non-broad-
casting use, as well as for school broadcast in adapted form.[22]

This recommendation, be it noted, is in line with the recommendations of the Commission on Instructional Technology,
which were considered earlier in this chapter. It is in line, also,
with proposals that President Nixon made early in 1970 to
Congress for the establishment of a National Institute of Education, with which the Corporation for Public Broadcasting
would work closely.

Many institutions and agencies exist here and there around
the country, now "playing solo," that could be brought to work
in concert to advance the use of technology in education, from
early childhood through the adult years. Among these are some
of the Research and Development Centers, the Regional Laboratories, and the Educational Resources Information Centers
(ERICs). Among these also are the National Instructional
Television Center, at Bloomington, Indiana, and the Centers
for Instructional Communications at Syracuse University, Indiana University, Michigan State University and the University
of Southern California. Several states have systems of "telecommunications" in varying stages of planning and development, such as the Colorado Commission on Educational Communications. Experience is being acquired, evaluated and com-
municated by such experiments as the Articulated Instructional
Media Program at the University of Wisconsin, using the full

range of communications media in the continuing education of adults.[23]

Thus solid reasons support the hope that the present depressing state of educational technology, including radio and television, in continuing education will improve.

However, that hope rests upon the assumption that the public broadcasting system, at all levels, will embrace continuing education as an integral part of its mission. Dr. James Zigerell, Dean of the highly successful TV College, Chicago City College, questions that assumption. He fears that the public television system, "like commercial TV, is about to slough off of its responsibilities by leaving a good deal of what it should be doing in organized adult and continuing education programmng to the humble instructional broadcasters, whose activities are to be confined to the closed-circuit hinterland."

He calls upon the practitioners of public television and adult and continuing education to join forces. He ends with the crucial question: "Will the leadership be found in time? Or has the cause already been lost?"[24]

Leadership from both fields and their cooperation will certainly be required, but one should recognize also the problem of air time. Much programming for the continuing education of adults through television should be available at a time when adults are home from work, which is also the prime time for the many other tasks that public broadcasting needs to perform for general audiences. Cable television may be the answer to this problem. Leadership, cooperation *and cable* may answer Zigerell's question, "No, the cause of adult and continuing education through television has not already been lost."

Relationships and Developments

The four areas where television for public purposes serves—broadcasting for general audiences, for children, for formal instruction, and for continuing education—are neither watertight compartments nor fully developed fields.

For example, much programming for general audiences in

cultural and public affairs can be used both for instruction and continuing education. Television for children, such as "Sesame Street," can be regarded in different ways—either as broadcasting to a special segment of the general audience, or as preinstructional broadcasting, or even as an early stage of continuing education. Some of the programs for formal instruction and some of the programs for continuing education, suitably adapted, can be used for both purposes.

The four areas where television for public purposes now serves are neither fully developed nor complete. Other purposes and objectives will emerge from the evolving needs of the people and the society, and from the evolving capabilities of the medium and other media. The tags put upon particular kinds of programming do not matter, so long as the public television system is sensitive to the needs of the people and responsive to opportunities to meet them.

The Public Television System and the People

What is the nature of the partnership between the broadcasting system and the people that must be established if the potentialities of television for public purposes are to be realized? This question has been answered operationally—with many illustrations—during the examination of each of the four areas where the public television system serves. Therefore the summary answer can be brief: The system should seek to serve the most important needs of all the people; the people should be encouraged and enabled to use the system as an instrument to accomplish their many purposes, both public and private.

The system of television for public purposes should be governed, managed and operated by men and women who care more for the world, for life and for people than they care for the medium of television. The system needs to develop a new kind of professionalism—one that can elicit, guide and develop the skills and talents of many kinds of people, institutions and agencies. The system of television for public purposes should be a social as well as an electronic medium—a medium for transmitting the talents, resources, energies and concerns of all the people to the entire community, in all its variety and on all its levels.

A list of the major purposes of the public television system, as they are now defined, will suggest the breadth and depth of the cooperation it must gain and cultivate: to renew a sense of community; to renew the social contract; to improve the people's internal environment; to help youngsters value learning and acquire basic skills; to become an integral part of formal instruction; to provide adults with opportunities for continuing their education; to serve the nation's priorities, particularly those that are not served by the dollar economy.

Both the people and the broadcasting system must regard television for public purposes as the people's instrument. The focus should be on goals, objectives, tasks, patterns of relationship and processes—not upon institutions. The requirement is that people of many kinds and concerns work together to make the most powerful means of communications serve the common good. Working together on present needs and with present opportunities will be to prepare to take advantage of the greater opportunities and capabilities that are already coming over the horizon.

1. *The Hidden Medium*, p. II-20.

2. "Television for the general public" is a phrase used by the Corporation for Public Broadcasting as one part of its all-inclusive term "Public Television." The Report of the Carnegie Commission on Educational Television uses "Educational Television" as the all-inclusive term, one part of which it calls "Public Television," meaning television for the general public. This book uses "television for general audiences" in the more restricted sense of the two other terms.

3. It should be noted that these objectives cut across the usual division of programming according to content—i.e., news, public affairs, political affairs, social affairs, the arts and humanities, etc., although, in general the first two objectives are likely mainly to involve news, public affairs, political affairs and social affairs, and the third objective is obviously more likely to involve the arts and humanities. Since content areas will be considered later, it is better at this stage to forget about content and to focus on objectives.

4. ". . . the problem of racism is not something that we can limit . . .
This is *our* problem. It is a countrywide problem, and a worldwide problem,
one that threatens to blast us to oblivion because we all feel threatened. . . . It
is realy a *human* problem, which means that maybe for the first time public
television can look at what the parameters, what the dimensions are, what
the depth of racism is. This seems to be something avoided in the universities,
avoided in the church, avoided in the political structure, avoided everywhere
you look. Public television may be the last major vehicle, the last voice, this
thing can have."—J. Alford Cannon, M.D., *Transcript of Proceedings, Kettering
Conference on Public Television Programming* (Dayton, Ohio: Charles F. Kettering Foundation, 1969), p. 54.

5. Harry Skornia, p. 179.

6. The author uses the phrase "cultural television" reluctantly, in lack of a
better one, hoping that his definitions and later illustrations will cleanse it of
patronizing or arrogant or elitist taints. "Television of the arts and humanities," besides being longer, would be no better, because neither "the arts"
nor "the humanities" can be well defined and even taken together they would
be too restrictive.

7. Judith Murphy and Ronald Gross, *The Arts and the Poor: New Challenge for Educators* (Washington, D.C.: prepared by the Academy for Educational Development, Inc., published by the U.S. Department of Health,
Education and Welfare, June 1968), pp. 17-18. This is a remarkable summary
of a remarkable conference conducted by the Brooklyn Museum November
15-19, 1966, in Gaithersburg, Maryland. It is filled with ideas and examples
of the vital role of art in the lives of all people, particularly the poor and
disadvantaged. It is recommended for the working library of every television
and radio station.

8. Rose Mukerji (Bloomington, Indiana: prepared for National Instructional
Television, with the aid of a planning committee, 1969).

9. See *Television and the Wired City*, pp. 99-101. The estimated costs of
evening-hour entertainment programs per week for ABC was $4,884,000; NBC,
$5,585,000; and for CBS, $4,964,000.

10. Early in 1970 Action for Children's Television, Boston, filed with the FCC,
and the commission accepted for study, a proposal that children's programs
be made part of the public service requirement of television stations and not
be commercially sponsored. This proposal reveals the limitations of commercial
television. If the children's programs are *not* sponsored, then the networks and
stations will be under economic pressures both to economize on the costs of
the programs for children and to reduce their other public-service programming.
If, on the other hand, the children's programs *are* sponsored, the high costs of
the programs will be paid by advertisers in the expectation of high returns.
Thus the children will be regarded primarily as "little consumers," not as
people in their own right. The purpose of the program will be to attract and to
hold audiences rather than to stimulate and to teach children.

11. "Television for instruction," or "instructional television" (ITV), or
"televised instruction," is much more complex than television for general audiences, including children. It is transmitted by three wireless techniques—

broadcasting (VHF and UHF), Instructional Television Fixed Service (ITFS-2500 megaherz radiation), and microwave (a point-to-point beam)—and two wired techniques—closed-circuit systems capable of multiplexing up to 82 (theoretically) channels on a single cable, and closed systems that can "coax" single-channel video signals of very high quality over relatively short distances. The instructional services and the roles of the educational stations in relationships with schools and colleges are at least as varied as the techniques of transmission. Such differences are not pertinent to the purposes of this book.

12. Quoted by Judith Murphy and Ronald Gross in *Learning by Television* (New York: written by the Academy for Educational Development, Inc., commissioned and published by The Fund for the Advancement of Education, 1966).

13. A survey conducted by the National Instructional Television Center, Bloomington, Indiana "One Week in Educational Television"—May 6-12, 1968, revealed that 45 percent of the total UHF/VHF broadcast hours of 152 stations were devoted to ITV and that all but five of the stations broadcast programs specifically for classrooms and/or academic credit.

14. See, for example, Judith Murphy and Ronald Gross, *op. cit.; The New Media and Education: Their Impact on Society*, edited by Peter H. Rossi and Bruce J. Biddle (Garden City, N.Y.: Anchor Books, Doubleday & Company, Inc., 1967); *Television in Instruction: What Is Possible*, National Association of Educational Broadcasters 1970; *Innovation in Education: New Directions for the American School* (New York: Committee for Economic Development, 1968); and Richard Hooper, "A Diagnosis of Failure," in *AV Communications Review*, Vol. 17, No. 3, Fall 1969.

15. *To Improve Learning*: A Report to the President and the Congress of the United States (Washington, D.C.: Academy for Educational Development, August 1969).

The history of this report is part of the history of the development of the public television system. The Carnegie Commission on Educational Television did not study instructional television but emphasized its potential importance and recommended that "federal, state, local and private educational agencies sponsor extensive and innovative studies to develop better insights into the use of television in formal and informal education." Title III of the Public Broadcasting Act of 1967 authorized the Secretary of Health, Education and Welfare "to conduct . . . a comprehensive study of instructional television and radio . . . and their relationship to each other and to instructional materials . . ." but this title was not funded. In March 1968 the secretary nevertheless appointed a nine-member Commission on Instructional Technology, which was given wide-ranging scope: "Every aspect of instructional technology and every problem which may arise in its development should be included." The study was intended to lead to action. "We have reached the point where we have simply got to come up with more orderly, informed way of taking advantage of all that the new technology has to offer." The commission selected the Academy for Educational Development to do the staff work.

16. "Adult education" is narrower than "the education of adults." The

latter includes all influences that have an impact on the adult mind; the former includes only those activities that are education by *intent*. "Continuing education" is a phrase that is replacing "adult education" because it connotes less of "catching up" and more of "keeping up," and it makes more explicit the notion of education as a life-long process; however, the two terms are usually used interchangeably, and often together.

17. Other examples could be cited. "Law Enforcement and Criminal Justice," produced by WGBH-TV, Boston, was carried on nineteen educational stations in the East and received by more than 25,000 law-enforcement officers in 500 federal, state and local agencies. WETA-TV, Washington, D.C., has produced and broadcast a basic Russian course for adults. For other examples in both radio and television, see Jack Crittenden Everly, *Continuing Education Instruction via the Mass Media*, a Ph.D thesis in communications, University of Illinois, Urbana, 1968. This study is recommended as a report, an analysis and a source of bibliographical and other reference.

18. James D. Carroll, "Science and the City: The Question of Authority," *Science*, Vol. 163 (February 28, 1969), p. 909.

19. Peter F. Drucker, *The Age of Discontinuity: Guidelines to Our Changing Society* (New York: Harper & Row, 1969), p. 323.

20. J. Eugene Welden, "30 Million Adults Go To School," *American Education*, November 1969. Welden is with the Division of Adult Education Programs of the U.S. Office of Education. He based his article on a sample taken by the U.S. Bureau of the Census in April 1969.

21. Stanley Moses, "The Learning Force: An Approach to the Politics of Education," and address delivered at the 1969 Annual Meeting of the American Political Science Association, New York City, Sept. 3, 1969. Moses is with the Educational Policy Research Center, Syracuse University.

22. See Edwin G. Cohen, "Continuing Public Education Broadcasting: Today and Tomorrow," *Educational Broadcasting Review*, February 1970.

23. Charles A. Wedemeyer and Robert E. Najem, *AIM: From Concept to Reality* (Syracuse, N.Y.: Syracuse University Press, 1969).

24. James Zigerell, "Television and Adult Education: Another Lost Cause?" E/IB, October 1969, pp. 12-14.

V

STATION FUNCTIONS
AND PROGRAMMING GOALS

If public broadcasting is to become an instrument that the people will use for their vital purposes, both the system and the people must keep attention focused, not on institutions or facilities, but on the basic functions the stations can perform in the communities and the basic goals they aim at in programming.

Station functions and programming goals are the subjects of the present chapter. From them the basic process of attaining specific objectives follows: the analysis of the needs and the characteristics of the potential audiences, the determination of specific responses from specific audiences desired to result from specific programming efforts, the design and production of programs, the promotion, the transmission (including the scheduling) of the program, the reception by specific audiences, and the evaluation of results. Therefore the subject of audiences is postponed until the next chapter. Both this and the next chapter treat subjects in terms of *broadcasting*, because radio too is an integral part, but their emphasis is on television.

Ten Functions and Goals

The deliberations of educational broadcasters and other groups have identified a range of functions the educational stations should perform in the community, or, to put the matter differently, a range of goals they should aim at in their programming. The functions and goals within this range are so interrelated as to be but various aspects of the same enterprise, which the Carnegie Commission summarized in the single word "freedom":

". . . We seek freedom from the constraints, however necessary in their context, of commercial television. We seek for edu-

83

cational television freedom from the pressures of inadequate
funds. We seek for the artist, the technician, the journalists,
the scholar, and the public servant freedom to create, freedom to
innovate, freedom to be heard in this most far-reaching medium.
We seek for the citizen freedom to view, to see programs that
the present system, by its incompleteness, denies him."[1]

Although freedom is indivisible, analysis and argument require
specifications. Therefore the following statements of station functions and programming goals are attempted. Illustrations are
given. Individually they date quickly; cumulatively they have
the disadvantage of looking backward in a book that seeks to
look ahead. But one cannot draw illustrations from what has
not yet come to pass. And a specific example of a station's function or of a station's programming goal *in action* at least "turns
them to shapes, and gives to airy nothing a local habitation and
a name."[2]

1. *To report and interpret public issues and to cover public affairs*

The function to be performed and the goal to be aimed at go
beyond mere information. Speaking to the National Press Club
on January 15, 1970, John W. Macy Jr., President of the Corporation for Public Broadcasting, described the task:

"I am convinced that the American people are now seeing
and reading *more* about the state of their nation than ever before,
and believe it *less*.

"It is not a case of 'credibility gap' between the people and
their government. It has become a veritable Grand Canyon of
disbelief involving not only government figures at national and
local levels, but the communicators who report on their actions
and the spokesmen who advocate public causes. . . .

". . . I believe this stems from a growing feeling on the part of
a substantial number of people that all public affairs are being
stage-managed for them—that their elected officials are images
to be marketed; that social issues are being orchestrated to produce the most potent impact on the media.

"They assume that communications about public thoughts

and deeds are designed and executed with the medium as the basic purposes. . . .

". . . none of this should be interpreted as criticism of the commercial networks or stations. By and large, they are doing—and doing very well indeed—what they must do under a system which measures survival and success in terms of mass-audience ratings that respond more to the stimulus of entertainment and excitement than to information. . . . But to expect them to provide sustained coverage of many sides of complicated public issues such as hunger, environmental destruction, or even a local school-bond controversy; to expect them to provide air time for citizens to become involved in these controversies, is to expect too much.

". . . I . . . offer a positive, upbeat alternative: public broadcasting. Because it is not fettered by the necessity of program ming for the greatest possible audience all the time, public broadcasting should be the vehicle used to return to the concept that through rational debate and discussion reasonable men can work to solve public issues; the vehicle to give the citizen some opportunity to make his own judgments known on these issues."

The task of public broadcasting is to provide *more*—more news (reporting, analysis, interpretation and opinion) in greater depth and from more sources; more representative journalism about, for and by the people and their activities that get neglected; more and deeper "slices of life" about the usual and the ordinary; more access to the primary experiences of hearings, deliberations and decision-making; above all, more credibility.

Here are some illustrations of such kinds of *more:*

National Educational Television had an extensive network program on the Vietnam Moratorium of October 15, 1969—an event almost ignored by the commercial networks. NET was first to accept Vice President Spiro Agnew's challenge that too many "liberal" viewpoints are heard from New York and Washington and not enough other viewpoints from elsewhere in the country; it had a network program titled "Middle America" televised at WTTW-TV, Chicago, involving four Midwest jour-

nalists and the "man in the street." The program was part of
the regular twice-a-month series "News in Perspective" produced jointly by NET and The New York Times. (The second
program each month is often produced outside of New York and
occasionally outside of the United States.)

The nationally televised "Washington Week in Review," produced by WETA-TV, Washington, D.C., emphasizes the background and long-range significance of events.

KQED-TV, San Francisco, broadcasts "Newsroom," an hour-
long program five days a week, during which the working newsmen in the station newsroom informally present and discuss
the whys and hows and meanings of the events they have
covered during the day; the mayor of the city has said he must
watch it to keep informed. Similar ventures have been funded
in several other cities, including Pittsburgh, Dallas and Washington, D.C.

At the request of the major of Berkeley, KQED-TV covered
the entire five-hour meeting of the City Council deliberating
what to do the next morning about the 1969 Memorial Day
march on the People's Park; the council's decision was a factor
in a peaceable solution; the coverage was state-wide over both
noncommercial and commercial stations, radio as well as television.

Through interconnections, KEBS-TV, San Diego, broadcast
a national special program on the Santa Barbara oil spill, and
KUON-TV, Lincoln, Nebraska, provided national coverage of a
Department of Agriculture hearing on farm problems.

Less than a month after the murder of Martin Luther King
Jr., NET coordinated the broadcasting over more than sixty
affiliated stations, including those in the largest cities, of a crash
program to help promote interracial understanding before the
end of the school year; "One Nation Indivisible?" funded by The
Ford Foundation, demonstrated that the public television system can respond quickly.

The educational television stations played a major role in the
information, discussion and debate that preceded Hawaii's
becoming a state; they regularly broadcast the activities of the

legislature. Coverage of the legislatures and governors, often with interviewing reporters, is a regular fare of the ETV stations in several other states as well, including Nebraska, South Carolina, Utah and Virginia. In 1968 the Florida ETV stations broadcast four one-hour programs of the candidates for the U.S. Senate, with a panel of reporters, and also two half-hour programs on which appeared the six candidates for the State Supreme Court. KUHT-TV, Houston, regularly broadcasts meetings of the school board. KCTS-TV, Seattle, and WHA-TV, Madison, telecast appearances of every candidate for municipal office. KCET-TV, Los Angeles, has presented all thirteen candidates for mayor. WHYY-TV, Philadelphia, covers the meetings of the city council. WGTV-TV, Athens, Georgia, broadcasts a statewide daily hour-long program on "The Growing South."

Such are some illustrations of what the public television system has already done on its frayed shoestring. One of the recommendations of the Study Group on the Mass Media of the National Commission on the Causes and Prevention of Violence, released January 12, 1970, was:

"That the Corporation for Public Broadcasting be provided with a budget for news and public affairs programming comparable to that of the television networks. The three networks spent about $150,000,000 for such programs last year. We believe that approximately $40,000,000 to $50,000,000 should be provided to the CPB for news and public affairs. The corporation should focus on providing those services which commercial broadcasting cannot or will not perform."[3]

2. To be an open forum for opinion, debate and discussion

In the Red Lion Case, the U.S. Supreme Court ruled that broadcasting is covered by the First Amendment for the purpose of preserving an "uninhibited market place of ideas," not to permit "monopolization of that market," whether by the government or by a private licensee. The First Amendment, the court decided, does not prohibit the Federal Communications Commission "from requiring a licensee to share his frequency with others and to conduct himself as a proxy or fiduciary with obligations to present those views and voices which would other-wise, by necessity, be barred from the airwaves."

But here, again, *more* is needed. To promote the full realiza-tion of the First Amendment, government must do more than refrain from abridging the people's right to a multitude of ideas and experiences; it must do more than try to enforce the fairness doctrine in commercial broadcasting. Commercial broadcasting cannot provide an adequate market place of *ideas* because it must live within the limitations of the *economic* market place. Government must do more. An important part of that *more* is to help support an alternative and supplementary system of broadcasting that has the affirmative purpose of stimulating the free market of ideas. For example:

During the 1969 student strike at Harvard University, WGBH-TV, Boston, devoted a total of seven hours of prime time during three successive evenings to broadcasting the full spectrum of arguments and opinions. That station also covered the entire hearings before the U.S. Commission on Civil Rights in Roxbury and the entire hearings before the Boston City Council on the recommendations of the Kerner Commission.

WCET-TV, Cincinnati, broadcasts a weekly half-hour pro-gram "Focus on Youth," which began before the death of Martin Luther King Jr. to give black teenagers a forum and then broadened its scope. It has also a regular program, "Meet the Man," that gives college students opportunity to argue with guest experts.

WJCT-TV, Jacksonville, has worked out a technique that pro-motes both expression and listening. It has used three locations for its "town meetings," switching from one to another, giving everyone a chance to speak in his own context. One meeting might be held in an exclusive club, another in a community hall in a poor district, and a third in the studio where the "experts" hold forth. Each group speaks and hears what the others are saying and has a chance to respond.

One of the most vigorous organizations using broadcasting to promote discussion, debate and study is Town Meeting, Inc., St. Paul, Minnesota. It has had programs in Brookings, South

Dakota; Fargo, North Dakota; and Morehead, Duluth, Superior and the Twin Cities, Minnesota. Some sixty half-hour television shows were produced and shown throughout the viewing areas. A study guide developed for the series was distributed to groups that continued their discussions.

National Educational Television regularly provides its affiliate stations with several series devoted to the fullest expression of the spectrum of opinions and designed to stimulate further discussion and debate. Among these have been "The Dissenters," a series of six weekly half-hour programs featuring personalities and voices from both the left and the right; "In My Opinion," a series of half-hour programs in which various public figures speak out on political and social issues; and the Foreign Policy Association's yearly "Great Decissions" series, which has supplementary study materials, and which for several years was seen nationally.

*   *   *

At the 1969 Kettering Conference on Public Television Programming, Charles Frankel, professor of philosophy at Columbia University, told the broadcasters:

"You have an obligation to try to get an audience that can imagine the adversary, imagine his reality, take him as he sees himself. This doesn't mean you have to agree with him, but at least understand that there is disagreement between human beings, not just magnify the hatred in the country."

Yes; the goal is not just to magnify the hatred in the country, or the fear, either. A question is How do you get a *government* that can imagine adversaries who are loyal citizens? that can take them as they see themselves and at least pay attention to their realities as they see them? How can you get a government that will accept the *necessary* adversary role in democracy? The answer is certainly not to remain silent, when silence is interpreted as assent, and massive silence as majority approval; certainly the answer is not to submit to the repression of your own dissent or to acquiesce, or even take part, in the silencing of the dissent of others.

Has the world become too complex for democracy? Considering the alternatives, the answer is No. The world has become
too complex for anything except a democracy that draws upon
the widest possible range of human experience, wisdom and talent. It has become too interdependent and fragile for anything
except self-government by a people who are aware and informed,
and who participate affirmatively.

3. *To provide means for participation in the making of public
decisions and the solution of problems.*
This task is integrally related to the two previous tasks.
Knowledge and understanding without opportunity to act increase frustration; action without knowledge and understanding,
sooner or later, is wrong action. The task of providing means
for participation has at least three levels: to give means to those
who have none, or none they know how to use; to improve the
procedures of decision-making and problem-solving; and to improve the quality of decisions and solutions.
Television in its present stage is not well developed to serve as
a means for participation. Technologically, it is still dominantly
a one-way medium. Psychologically, it is still regarded as primarily a medium for entertainment and commerce. Sociological-
ly, the people who are most dependent upon television for their
information, ideas and attitudes are the ones who are most
passive in their approach to political and social problems; they
are also the ones least likely to watch serious television (except
what touches their close interests) , and they are even less likely to use it as an instrument for participation (with the same
exception) .
Nevertheless, the need to provide means for citizen participation is critical—to given an alternative to the apathy of hopeless-
ness, on the one hand, and to the recklessness of despair, on the
other hand; to make the vast, impersonal institutions of the
American society more human and more responsive. The need
is critical to engage the hopes and to harness the talents and
energies of great numbers of people who are left out—both those
who never have had opportunity to take active part in self-

government and those who are now being squeezed out by the tightening coil of concentrating, self-serving power.

Although television in its present stage is not well developed to give a means for citizen participation, its potentialities to do so are great. They can become much greater with larger technological capacities and with experimentation and experience.[4]

Most of the ways by which public television widens citizen participation and makes institutions more responsive are indirect—through a raising of the level of awareness and concern and through the many channels that public opinion and will make themselves felt. But here and there, now and then, public television demonstrates how it can directly serve as a means to widen participation and quicken responsiveness.

A bond issue for urban renewal in mostly Negro slum areas was voted down in Harrisburg, Pennsylvania. WITF-TV, Hershey, which serves Harrisburg, then held a series of live televised public meetings. Afterwards the voters reversed their decision.

The Utah state television stations have the regular program "Goals for Utah" with two-way telephone connections that stimulates wide participation.

Many other ETV stations are deeply committed to community involvement in decision-making and problems solving, particularly those in Los Angeles, San Francisco, Madison, Pittsburgh, Syracuse, Boston and Jacksonville.

"Crisis in Congo" suggests that role-playing, simulation and games have large potentialities for teaching and practicing decision-making and for good television as well. "Crisis" was a series of five live half-hour television programs on consecutive Thursdays in early 1969 over twenty-six stations affiliated with the Eastern Educational Network. High school students in five New England states played the diplomatic role of China, students in five New York State cities played the role of the United States, students in Washington, D.C., and the Pennsylvania cities played the role of the Soviet Union. Students watching the game in twenty-six cities afterwards carried on debates and voted on problems or questions. The votes were fed back to affect negotiations in the following weeks. The game was developed by three high school students who concluded that they could devise a game better than the Eastern Educational Network game "Cabinet in Crisis," which they had played.

"The Advocates" is another format that illustrates the imaginative use of television to promote reasoned discussion and participation in decision-making and to result in good programmng as well. Each Sunday night over interconnections, an important national issue is debated in the manner of a judicial hearing. There are advocates, a "judge," officials who actually must make decisions on the issue being discussed, experts, examinations and cross-examination. Then the studio audience and the viewers everywhere are asked to register their opinions, which are forwarded by the stations to the appropriate decision-makers. The national series is produced by and originates from KCET-TV, Los Angeles, and WGBH-TV, Boston. Responses from viewers registering their "votes" on a single program have exceeded 14,000.

NET televised the White House Conference on Food, Nutrition and Health in December 1969. In addition, CPB supported local programs by twelve stations for broadcasting community discussions of food and nutrition problems. The tapes of these local programs were sent to officials of the White House Conference.

This last example touches the boundaries of two largely unexplored continents of possibilities. One is the tying in of special national television programs with important national meetings, such as the annual conference of the American Association for the Advancement of Science. The other is the relating of television programs with organized study-discussion-action groups. (This latter potentiality will be developed in Chapter Eight, "Serving Priorities.")

*   *   *

The chief virtue of self-government is that it is *educative.* Thinking always starts with some kind of difficulty or problem or unresolved situation. It develops as a person has the opportunity to grapple with the difficulty, problem or situation. The capacity to be responsibly free, or freely responsible, is one that can be developed only with exercise. A main strength of the American democracy at earlier stages in its history was that the institutions and agencies of self-government permitted—indeed, required—people to use them, and to grow in the use. A main difficulty in the American society today is that many of our institutions and procedures no longer permit, and much less require, wide participation; consequently, opportunities for the people to learn and to grow are denied. To the degree that public television provides means for participation in decision-making and problem-solving, to that degree it will also be educative of our citizenry. To that degree it will also be helping to create new forms and procedures of self-government appropriate to our highly institutionalized society.

4. To perform important public services

Some of the important public services that public television can perform are ordinary and continual, like that of the South Carolina ETV Network's "Job Man Caravan," whose mobile unit goes to a different place each week with phones to receive information about job opportunities and equipment to broadcast the job-seekers' skills. Some of the services it can perform are dramatic and unexpected, like that of WGBH-TV after the death of Martin Luther King Jr. A rock concert by black folk-singer James Brown was scheduled. The authorities of Boston feared the assembly of 15,000 teenagers. Following saturation radio announcements that the concert would be *televised*, WGBH-TV broadcast the program live and then repeated it the next day at 2.00 a.m. Boston was one of the few large cities that had no riot those two days.

Some of the services public broadcasting can perform are significant because they indicate large and opening areas that can be developed. Several illustrations follow.

During the last week of March 1970, the public television system's interconnections broadcast a complete four-day courtroom trial in four ninety-minute segments produced by NET.

"Trial—The City and County of Denver vs. Loren B. Watson," the first courtroom trial to be filmed for television, has long-range significance on several levels.

On one level, it opens again the question, should courtroom trials be covered by television? In 1965 the U.S. Supreme Court reversed the conviction of Billie Sol Estes on the ground that televising parts of his trial, over his objections, had deprived him of his right to due process under the Fourteenth Amendment. The majority of the court, going beyond the fact that the defendant had objected to the televising, ruled that the "evil of television" lies "in the trial participants' awareness that they are being televised." However, the Sixth Amendment guarantees the right to a "public trial." Are the trial participants not aware of the presence of the "public," including reporters for the print media? What does "public trial" mean in an electronic age? Where lies the "evil of television" when videotape is being used in some places as part of the court record? Speaking for the minority of four justices on the court, Byron R. White was unwilling to bar all forms of TV coverage because "currently available materials assessing the effect of cameras in the courtroom are too sparse and fragmentary." NET's "Trial" was a landmark demonstration that unobtrusively filming a trial for televising it later, with the assent of all parties, need not interfere with due process or the decorous conduct of that trial.

The national presentation of "Trial," a year after the trial took place, gave the American people their most intimate view into the workings of one of their fundamental processes of government. It will be a continuing national resource for popular education in the intricacies of truth, law, order and justice.

"Trial" was first presented to the American people the week before the U.S. Supreme Court ruled that juvenile courts may not convict children unless they are found guilty "beyond a reasonable doubt," as in the trials of adults. That decision was the first time the high court declared that juveniles are entitled to be judged by a strict burden of proof, but it reaffirmed a 1967 ruling that the safeguards of the Bill of Rights must protect the accused when his liberty is at stake whether his trial is labeled criminal or civil, punitive or rehabilitory. Thus the service that public television performed—and will continue to perform—in advancing the people's understanding of due process and tests of permissible evidence is of basic importance to all the American people, particularly those who have least protection. As Robert M. Fresco, the producer of "Trial," said: ". . . the law is too important to be left to lawyers alone. It is a system that needs looking at, and to keep it clouded in secrecy is a disservice to the legal system . . . It is completely possible that you can formalize public access to the courts without having a circus." [5]

*   *   *

A second large public service area now opening up to the public broadcasting system is that of acting as "unofficial ombudsman." Some of the possibilities were first demonstrated by the weekly program "The Hour Has Seven Days," broadcast for two years by the Canadian Broadcasting Corporation.[6] In 1969 the American Corporation for Public Broadcasting made a grant to WCNY-TV, Syracuse, to conduct a national pilot project that, it is hoped, will enable other public television stations to take on the ombudsman function and programming goal. With the grant and with local funds, the station employed a Citizen Advocate (an advanced student in the School of Law at Syracuse University) to handle the complaints of individual citizens about government action or inaction. In January 1970 the station began broadcasting a weekly half-hour program on the Citizen Advocate's work, consisting of reports on the issues, the investigations and the solution, as well as shots and film segments concerning the background and the protagonists. Thomas Petry, then manager of WCNY-TV, said "the intent of the program is to identify those problems and issues that exist within the community, to examine them in detail, and to seek to draw together those elements of the community that can effectively work together to bring about change . . . "

An ombudsman activity and program must be scrupulously honest and careful. Many newspapers and commercial broad-

casting stations have "action" features, but the main purpose
of many (perhaps most) of these is to attract readership or
audiences, not to serve the public. Newspapers and stations
with such self-serving intent select cases to grab interest or to
"show their muscle"; they often use, subtly or not, the threat of
bad publicity to get "results" and to get credit for getting "results."

An honest and careful ombudsman service is, therefore, costly to provide. One way by which public television stations
might be able to bear the expense is suggested by the "Call to
Action" project of the National Urban Coalition. Early in 1970,
Chairman John W. Gardner announced that his project would
be expanded to twenty-two cities. He said it "combines the
reach of radio and the power of the people." The stations urge
listeners to call for assistance. The calls are taken and followed
up by volunteers. The coalition sponsors and partially subsidizes
the project (by training the volunteers and reimbursing them for
expenses), but the main contributions are the efforts of the
volunteers. This arrangement suggests that if public television
stations are to assume the ombudsman role and to extend such
services very far, they must seek to achieve the "multiplier-
effect" of cooperation with many other agencies and organizations and with private citizens.

Properly done, the ombudsman service has an influence far
beyond the relatively few cases it can handle. Speaking of the
experience of the Canadian series "Every Hour Has Seven
Days," Douglas Leiterman, who produced it, said:

". . . every time you run a case, there is a sense that flows
through that country, through that audience that somebody
up there cares. . . .

". . . Every time you do a case, you are deluged by hundreds
and thousands of other people who have complaints. . . . But
the important thing was not that we get a lot of that kind of
response, but that every time one little guy had his piece, the
kinds of oppressive bureaucracy that we all suffer from was given
pause. Bureaucrats had to think twice because they saw what

had happened to one of their number on a preceding program; and the little people decided that maybe they could fight, too."[7]

*   *   *

A movement in Europe shows the tie between the previous public service and still another that public television can perform: The Scandinavian and other countries in Western Europe are extending the role of ombudsman to protect the *consumer*. Examples of American public television programs designed to inform consumers could be cited, such as the NET monthly "Your Dollar's Worth" series, which presented objective reports on the quantity and prices of specific goods and services; the March 1970 NET series "Why You Smoke—A Self Test,"[8] and numerous programs by local stations. But we can more profitably pay attention to larger needs and opportunities revealed by current trends.

The tide of dissatisfaction by American consumers rose constantly during the 1960's. In October 1969 President Nixon told Congress: "Consumerism—Upton Sinclair and Rachel Carson would be glad to know—is a healthy development that is here to stay." Those two crusaders are dead, in a way, but Ralph Nader and his Raiders are not dead in any way. The exposures they and many others have made reveal not only malpractices but also the limitations of regulation, whether "voluntary" through codes, or "mandatory" through government agencies. Both business corporations and government agencies have twitched in response, but whatever protection the consumer will get in the long run (Upton Sinclair and Rachel Carson could tell us) must be solidly based upon widespread knowledge and effective organization.

In general, the American people as consumers do not know what is in their food, how much interest they pay, whether "cheap" products are really cheap or even safe. They are not well informed about the hazards that are run, both by special groups, such as coal miners, and by everybody, such as drivers and passengers in automobiles. What they do know they have

not learned from the makers and sellers. As consumers, the
American people have no organization to champion their interests effectively in the arena with the manufacturers, purveyors
and advertisers.

Here, then, is a large area of public service for public television. Large as it is, it is only the foyer to even larger areas of
public services that the American people need: to pass and
execute federal, state and local laws protecting the poor and
ignorant from the gougings that fuel discontent and revolt; to
give the American people the knowledge and organization to assert the general interest against the push and pull of such special
interests as the lobbies for business, agriculture, labor and communications; first to halt and then to reverse the destruction of
the environment (Houston to Apollo 13: "We've got to preserve our consumables."); to change huge, powerful, rigid institutions so as to meet the practical and moral imperatives for
a better society.

By itself alone, public television can perform none of these
larger services, of course, but none of them can be performed
by any combination of efforts without the essential service of
public education that can be provided only by a system of broadcasting devoted to the public interest.

*5. To help the various parts of the community better under-
stand themselves, one another and their community*

Another function the public broadcasting system can perform—another goal for its programming—is to enable the many
groups that make up our society to communicate, each to itself and to the others. This function and goal cannot be stated
precisely because basic questions are unanswered: What is
"the community"? What is the nature of America?

The American past, present and future can be regarded in
one of two ways, according to Louis Adamic: first, as an Anglo-
Saxon civilization struggling to preserve itself against adultera-
tions; or, second, as a fabric woven of threads from many cultures, with diversity itself the pattern.

"Perhaps we in the United States are today in somewhat the

same state of being, of thinking and feeling that existed before
the world's roundness altered the flat, cramped horizons of men's
minds. Millions of American's all sorts of them, sense the inade-
quency of the first way of looking at America. . . .

". . . But the statement Diversity itself is the pattern of
America will remain a rather chilly formula until we become
aware of the abundant details which give it life, until we know
more about the experiences and qualities, hopes and achievements of the many kinds of people who have made America.
Not until wave after wave of these facts sweeps over us, startles
us, rouses our interest, will the second view, or something very
like it, ring in the American atmosphere, the American consciousness." [9]

Adamic took his title, "A Nation of Nations," from Walt
Whitman's preface to *Leaves of Grass*. Whitman wrote that
preface in 1855, amid the gathering storm that nearly destroyed
the United States. Adamic wrote his book in 1945, amid the
gathering storm from which the United States either will not
emerge as a nation or will emerge as a "nation of nations."
What Adamic described as the "inadequacy" of the Anglo-
Saxon view of American civilization, the National Commission
on the Causes and Prevention of Violence a quarter of a century
later described as the "myth of the melting pot" obscuring a
flaw that will be fatal if it is not removed.

One aspect of America as Diversity is ethnic—Negroes, yes,
but also Indians, Chicanos, Puerto Ricans, various kinds of
Oriental-Americans, and beyond this, a multitude of ethnic
white minorities. Many ethnic minorities are now cohering, and
all for the same reason: Group identity gives a person a measure
of supporting self-acceptance and self-esteem; group organization gives a measure of power. They have all learned well a
esson from American history—that no minority group ever
chieved acceptance through dependence upon the benevolence
of the dominant society.

The concept of ethnicity could be fashioned into an excuse
for racial discrimination ("*They want* to be by themselves").
Historian John Hope Franklin has put the point this way: "If

the history of ethnicity has meant anything at all during the last
three centuries, it has meant the gradual retreat from the broad
and healthy regard for cultural and racial differences to a narrow,
a counter-productive concept of difference in terms of whim,
intolerance and racial prejudice."

Perhaps we need a different word to connote the "broad and
healthy regard for cultural differences" that does not compromise
basic principles of equality and justice. Regardless of words, the
ideal is clear. The ideal of integrity with justice is significant
to all of us.

The ideal of integrity with justice is significant to all ethnic
minorities, of course. It is significant also to minorities whose
bond are not primarily racial: to those who found George Wal-
lace a spokesman for their sense of being wronged; to women;
to the young; to the old, and so on and on. The ideal is significant
to people who are bound together by the fact of their living together in geographical regions, or in types of localities (rural,
urban, suburban, exurban) and so on and on. The ideal is significant to the society as a whole because the governance of the
society depends upon the consent of the governed.

However, the One does not come from the Many without a
commonality of values, goals, power, respect and procedures.
The *resultant* of narrow contending forces does not lead to the
common good without a saving measure of broad rationality and
common concern.

"The interplay, the diversity, is America; all that lacks is to
transplant the fact from obscurity into the American imagination. The rest will pretty much take care of itself, for the read-
justment in thinking and feeling will reach into every phase of
American activity." [10]

Public television has begun to transplant the fact of diversity from obscurity into the American imagination. The examples are, encouragingly, too many even to list. They include
NET's nine-program series "History of the Negro People" and
the continuing magazine-format "Black Journal"; "Soul!" of
WNDT-TV, New York, the only weekly black program broadcast nationally; the original dramas of WGBH-TV, Boston, "On

Being Black;" "Black Voices of KTCA-TV, Minneapolis-St. Paul; "Bird of the Iron Feathers," by WTTW-TV, Chicago; "CPT" (Colored People's Time), WTVS-TV, Detroit; "Black Frontier," of KUON-TV, Lincoln; "Our Kind of World," the series of "soap operas" using a black family and a Spanish-American family by KRMA-TV, Denver; the programs in English and Spanish on Cuban immigrants by WTHS-TV, Miami; the broadcasts by remote pickups from the barrios of Austin and San Antonio by KLRN-TV; and "Cancion de la Raza" of KCET-TV, Los Angeles.

Some programs such as these, presented locally or nationally, are designed to give minorities a means of expressing themselves to themselves; some are designed to speak to general audiences. The emphasis has been upon black Americans, but the public television system is broadening its concern.

Only when the American society recognizes the needs and rights of all minorities, only when it tries to help the members of all the lower classes and lower-middle classes to identify and solve their problems will the stresses of Diversity transcend division and support Unity.

White on white, black on black, red on red, women on women, young on young, old on old—such analyses are necessary for self-expression and mutual understanding. But the synthesis of differences requires more. People of all kinds must speak and listen to each other about their common concerns for their common good. A task of the public broadcasting system, therefore, is to strengthen the valencies of the whole society by transforming into vivid realization the basic *conditions* that enable different kinds of people to live together and the basic *principles* that must govern their relationships.

6. *To further the American people's understanding of other peoples and of the world*

The idea behind another function the public broadcasting system serves in the community and another goal for its programming is profoundly simple: to help the American people better understand the human community we all belong to and the planet that is our home—our only, our threatened home.

The commercial media, particularly television, cover well, sometimes superbly, the dramatic event and the sensational crisis. But the commercial media do not cover well, sometimes do not cover at all, the background, the context, the meaning—least of all, the human meaning. Where there is no crises, on commercial broadcasting there usually is no "news." But, even though there is no crisis, Calvin Stillman, a director of the Broadcasting Foundation of America, told a Senate subcommittee, still:

". . . there is life, and struggle, and meaning, and hope, and hard work, and ways of life very hard for us to appreciate . . .

". . . to know the world is to know yourself—and to know yourself is a source of pride, and with pride comes a determination to make one's own culture as good a place to live in as one can.

". . . we must have more sources of in-depth information from other lands; fresh information, as much as possible in the words of the residents of other lands themselves. We should be hearing arguments and criticisms of ourselves—these will force us to consider ourselves and thus reaffirm our own standards of what is right, and of what are our responsibilities." [11]

In programming about other peoples and other parts of the world, local television stations are heavily dependent upon national sources. A few examples of the programming that the stations have received follow.

National Educational Television's program "Who Speaks for Man?" graphically contrasted the major issues that face the world with the inadequacy of the United Nations to deal with them.

On April 22, 1970. NET devoted its entire scheduling to "Earth Day" programming. That day even the children's programs—"Sesame Street," "Misterogers" and "What's New"—pertained to pollution.

"World Press,' a weekly review of press opinions around the globe, produced by KQED-TV, San Francisco, is broadcast nationwide.

Over the years NET has broadcast foreign assessments of U.S. foreign policy; hour-long excerpts of testimony before the Senate Foreign Relations Committee by such persons as Henry Steele Commager, John Gavin, George Kennan and Edwin Reischauer; and major documentary films made "on location" in such countries as Indonesia, Germany, France, Japan, Israel, South Africa, India, Great Britain, Spain, Burma, Thailand, Jordan, Ethiopia, Cuba, the U.S.S.R. and Rumania.

"International Magazine," a monthly hour-long NET series of selected films, reported on events and issues around the world; they were designed to give American viewers an understanding of the problems, attitudes and ways of life of other peoples.

"Spectrum," a national weekly NET science series, dealt with such subjects as human aggression, explorations in Antarctica and on the ocean floor, irrigation in the Negev desert, and the birth of the world.

In 1970 NET commissioned programs to examine man's relationship to the machine, the vanishing wilderness and the environment.

Some of the programs were "hot." NET presented a film on North Vietnam despite the protests of thirty-three members of the House of Representatives. "A Glimpse of China," a documentary film in China by a Canadian Broadcasting Corporation team, was broadcast only after an argument was won with the U.S. Customs officials at La Guardia airport. Several of the public television stations chose not to show "Who Invited Us?"—an hour-long documentary critical of U.S. foreign policy.

*   *   *

Such examples of programming designed to further an understanding of other peoples and of the world are but forerunners of much greater resources in the future. NET (the only U.S. participant) took part in, contributed to and broadcast the first round-the-world simultaneous television program transmitted by satellite in 1967. Titled "Our World," it linked up fourteen nations on five continents in a two-hour program. The

Corporation for Public Broadcasting is cooperating with NASA in experiments on the use of domestic satellites and is working closely also with other agencies on the uses of regional and world satellite systems. As the capabilities of interconnections are expanded, the public broadcasting system will be able more effectively to help the American people understand other peoples and the planet Earth.

7. *To improve our psychic environment*

One of the objectives of the public broadcasting system (set forth in the previous chapter) is to improve the people's internal environments. The intent of that phrase is to suggest, not "cultural uplift" for a few, but an essential service to *all* the people. Our psychic environments are as important as our physical environments. From them can come the visions of an external world that is more orderly, beautiful and humane.

This section on the function that cultural television (however unsatisfactory that phase may be) can perform in the community and on its programming goals will give examples to illustrate three points: First, cultural television is broad, deep and varied; second, it provides a means for artists to express themselves and gain publics as well as a means for publics to experience and appreciate the arts; and, third, it is also a means whereby public television performs some of its other functions and approaches some of its other goals.

*   *   *

Cultural television is "NET Playhouse," which ranges from *Uncle Vanya* to *Lizzie Borden;* it is "Is Somebody There?"— a program about what it means to be poor, fashioned from the writings of Carl Sandburg, Gordon Parks and Charles Baudelaire (WITF-TV, Hershey).

Cultural television is the "Sounds of Summer," which includes Arlo Guthrie and Pablo Casals and moved from the Berkshire Festival at "Tanglewood" in Massachusetts to the Illinois State Fair at DuQuoin; it is the programs produced at the 1969 summer National Youth Music Institute, participated in by the big-name rock groups and by high school music students and teachers from forty cities in the United States and England (WHA-TV, Madison).

Cultural television is ballet from Lincoln Center and jazz from Memphis.

Cultural television is "NET Opera;"[12] also it is a series on Arkansas folk music (KETS-TV, Little Rock).

Cultural television is "NET Festival"; it is the series on black folklore (WTVI-TV, Charlotte).

Cultural television is "The Forsyte Saga"; it is "On Being Black," a series of original dramas written by and starring blacks (WGBH-TV, Boston); it is "The Show," by and for teenagers (WITF-TV, Hershey); it is "Civilisation," the British thirteen-week art series produced by the British Broadcasting Corporaton and acquired by NET.[13]

Cultural television is "Book Beat" (WTTW-TV, Chicago); it is actress Bernice Avery reading Langston Hughes' poems on "CPT" (Colored People's Time, WTVS-TV, Detroit).

Cultural television is "In Search of Rembrandt"; it is "Nebraska in the 1870's," produced from still photographs (KUON-TV, Lincoln); it is the still photographs of John Tweedle touched to life by the moving cameras of WTTW-TV, Chicago.

Cultural television is insights into the cultures of other peoples through their writers and actors, their sculptors and painters, their musicians and architects; it is the 1970 project "Artist in America," to which all the public television stations in the United States were invited to contribute.

Cultural television is all these, and more. It is new kinds of documentary films, such as "Hospital", produced by Frederick Wiseman, with his rare talent, and such as may come from grants the Corporation for Public Broadcasting has made for films for television. It is the new forms and styles that may emerge from the National Center for Television Experiments (KQED-TV, San Francisco).

Cultural television is too free for some people and not free enough for others. Jac Venza, executive producer for drama,

NET, told the Kettering Conference on Public Television Programming: "We're talking about building popularity and building mass audiences. Let's think a little about what we'll be losing . . . And especially I'm concerned about kinds of artists who are going to get lost in the shuffle—artists who are the shapers of our intellectual future, who are the rabble-rousers of the mind. These are the artists who are going to force change, and these are just the ones we should attract. Whether their ideas are popular or not, they should be heard on public television." [14]

Melvin Tumin, professor of sociology and anthropology, Princeton University, stated another consideration:

". . . For a number of purposes important to art, at least some of those who are indifferent must come to care, some who disbelieve must come to share some faith, and some of those who are hostile must be persuaded to be more friendly . . .

"Some effective way must be found in which to test out some of the claims of art. . . . We need, crucially, vitally, above all, to find out, through sound research and evaluation, how good our ideas are, and, when and if their worth is established, how they can best be disseminated and multiplied so as to reach the widest possible audience. So the arts must prove their case, or continue to remain inconsequential and tangential to the mainsteam of experience in which our school children and, of course, our adult population will be exposed." [15]

Tumin was speaking, not about cultural television, but about the role of the arts in the American society. One of the purposes of public television is to advance the idea that the arts are as organic a part of American life as science and technology.

Somehow public television must build a tension bridge between the artists and the society. It must push toward the goal of giving the widest possible access both by artists to the people and by the people to the artists. It must give a chance by taking a chance. It must widen both freedom of expression and freedom of reception. It must expand the freedom of the American people to choose—and the greatest dimension of freedom is knowing, because the choice one cannot make is the choice one does not know exists.

8. *To help the American people cultivate the critical ability to use, not to be used by, the mass media*

The American people depend upon the media of mass communications, particularly television, for most of their perceptions of the vast, impersonal world they live in. They get the raw materials of second-hand or imaginary experience that influence their values, attitudes, goals and opinions. Many people, inside and outside of the media, relentlessly and skillfully try to make such power serve their own purposes. Their manipulation, delving deeper than the mass media, fashion and stage-manage many of the "events" that the mass media portray. Yet the American people get almost no help in developing the critical skills that will serve their own interests rather than the interests of those who would manipulate them.

The American people are sceptical of the news media. For example, a Gallup Poll released early in 1970 indicated that only 40 per cent of the people said the television networks present the news fairly and only 37 percent said the same about newspapers. Gallup reports that for the last several years more people say they trust the fairness of news over radio and television than say they trust the news in newspapers; to the extent that their trust is greater in the electronic news, this is a measure of the greater responsibility of these media. Much of the public scepticism of all the news media is unreasoned, as another nation-wide poll taken about the same time indicated: Responding to questions put by Columbia Broadcasting News, 55 per cent of those interviewed said that newspapers, radio and television should not be permitted to report stories considered by the government to be harmful to the national interest.

The commercial media do not help the American people develop critical abilities that would counteract their powers. The media do not report well news about their own affairs, if, indeed, they report it at all. The several media shun fundamental criticisms of one another. Such self-serving favoritism can be expected to increase as the interlocks of ownership and management tighten.

Occasional books analyze the structure and performance of the media of mass communications. So do a few scholarly journals, such as the *Columbia Journalism Review*. Now there is the *Chicago Journalism Review,* written and published by the "working stiffs" of the press; similar critiques are being planned in a few other cities.[16] A flood of the "underground press" is roiling. But none of these efforts reach many people; none concentrates on television; none either has or serves the purpose of broad public education.

No good printed materials designed for the general public exist.[17] American schools do not teach how to receive television critically.[18] The study group on mass media of the National Commission on the Causes and Prevention of Violence recommended that an independent national center be established to monitor and issue reports on the performance of the news media. Even if the proposal fares better than did a similar proposal made in 1948 by the Commission on Freedom of the Press, the effectiveness of such a center would require a widespread popular concern and a high level of public criticism.

The ability to criticize intelligently the way television handles news is only a part of the critical abilities that the people need in order to use television for their own purposes. They need to be able to go beneath the elementary questions ("Is this reporting, background, interpretation, opinion, advertising, argument? Who is talking? For whom? When and from where? What are the sources?" etc.) into a realm of much more subtle questions, such as: What are the underlying assumptions of the television program, whether news, documentary, advertising or entertainment? What attitudes or values does it favor or discourage? Do these attitudes and values serve the public good?

If self-government is to survive, the American people must learn how to use, rather than to be used by, the mass media, particularly television. Indeed, these media are a kind of government and a means for all other kinds of government that the people must be able to control, at least to the extent that they are not unwitting accomplices in their own subjection.

The survival of self-government requires a "new breed" of citizens and consumers, versed in the issues, practiced in dissent, mistrustful of established power and influence, who can throw off the hands that would manipulate them, tear off the masks that would deceive them, pierce through the "images" to the realities, and make their own judgments on solid rational grounds.

No institution or agency is helping the American people learn how to use the mass media. Therefore the task of giving leadership falls upon the public television system. Unfortunately, we must end the discussion without examples. The public television system has not even begun to assume this function in the community or to set this goal for its programming.

*   *   *

If the public television system has a responsibility to give leadership in helping the American people develop immunity to manpulation by the mass media, it must not itself try to manipulate the people. This simple axiom disposes of the ideas that public television should be an instrument for social engineering or a weapon for social revolution. We need say no more about the pretentiousness of any group that aspires to be engineers for the society, or about the rapid disintegration of the public television system that would follow any attempt to engineer or subvert.

The ideas can be quickly dismissed. However, two thoughts remain, not as qualifications in the rejection of those functions and goals, but as reminders for the public television system in its other activities.

One: Although the publc television system does not have social engineering as a goal, it does aim to become a powerful influence. This influence will have some effects. What are the effects the system wants to achieve?

Two: Although the public television system is not an agent for social revolution, vast and rapid changes in the American

society are bound to occur. What changes does the public
television system want to help, and what changes does it want
to hinder?

These questions will not go away with the easy dismissal
of social engineering and social revolution as appropriate goals.
The answer to them probably is that the public television system
will best serve the American people if it supports and advances
evolutionary changes in line with American ideals. It can do
so best, not by trying to "engineer" changes, but by helping the
American people achieve the awareness, the knowledge, the
understanding, the discourse of discussion and debate, the means
for coming to their own conclusions and for working together.
To the degree that it fails to perform this function, it will be
reinforcing the tendencies and behaviors that will result in violent
revolt and violent suppression.

9. *To act as a catalyst in making American education more
effective and more widely accessible*

The functions and programming goals of the public television
system in education cannot be stated precisely because education is the responsibilty of other institutions and agencies. Moreover, the relations between the public television system and
the American public school system have reached a crisis—a
stage of turning for better or worse.

As it has been used to date, instructional television cannot
upgrade American education; it can only alleviate some of the
problems caused by too many students, proliferating curricula
and too little money. As the schools have used and supported
instructional television to date, they cannot upgrade television
for public purposes; they can only alleviate some of the problems
created by having too little money, too few programs and too
few viewers. This fragile, mutually palliative relationship is
endangered by the responses that public education is making
to the bind it is in.

The institutions of primary, secondary and higher education
are caught up in a clash, as between mighty ice floes driven
together by a gale. Costs continue to mount. Demands for

more and better services to more and more different kinds of people continue to rise. The taxpayers' revolt spreads.

The institutions of primary, secondary and higher education respond to this squeeze with "more of the same." They try to keep more and more people in school for more and more years. They use their traditional methods of teaching, resorting to television, if at all, mostly to bring one classroom into another, or one lecturer into larger classes. When "economies" are made, instructional television, along with adult education, is among the first "frills" to be cut out.

But the fundamental problems of the American educational system cannot be solved by such "economies." Peter Drucker has diagnosed one of them:

"Teaching is the only major occupation of man for which we have not yet developed tools that make an average person capable of competence and performance. But education will be changed, because it is headed straight into a major economic crisis. It is not that we cannot afford the high costs of education; we cannot afford its low productivity. We must get results from the tremendous investment we are making." [19]

Stanley Moses has diagnosed another fundamental problem of the American educational system:

"The challenge to public policy in the future will be to innovate new programs and experiences which afford opportunities for growth and development in manners not afforded by the traditional educational system.

". . . Little attention has been given to the needs of people at all stages of life for different educational experiences. Little attention has been given to the needs of youth for direct personal experiences before reaching middle age. A more flexible educational system would be organized around the changing needs of both youth and adults and would offer opportunities for entrance and exit at different periods in life, with less need placed upon formalized credentials as prerequisites for participation. . . .

". . . What is needed is a fresh look at other forms of education outside the traditional system and the ways in which they can contribute to public policy and educational planning—

planning which will start with the needs of people and not institutions; of those who are served and not solely the professionals who control the service." [20]

Like the American educational system, the American governmental system—from the federal to the local levels—is also caught in a bind. President Nixon has announced that he wants to take a "new look" at how best to do what the nation wants in education, from pre-school through continuing education. He wants, in particular, to explore ways of making the educational system more "accountable" through research, planning and assessment; and more effective through the use of educational technology.

Educational technology is more than gadgetry. It is a way of thinking as much as a way of doing. It is a way of analyzing, organizing and managing education as a system, not of *institutions,* but of *elements;* as a *process,* not as a *product.* In this sense educational technology can provide a central means for implementing an integrated approach to educational planning and development, from pre-school through the primary, secondary and higher schools, and into continuing education.

Instructional television is an important part of educational technology. It can leap over barriers of segregation, whether de jure or de facto. It can diminish some of the differences between the conditions of rural, urban and suburban areas. It can narrow some of the financial gaps between poor districts and rich districts. It can help make mass education quality education. It can multiply the master teacher and the rare piece of equipment. It can bring the world into the classroom, including the world *now.*[21]

The public television system, including television for children, television for instruction and television for continuing education, is the only educational system that is in direct touch with all levels of government and with all levels and phases of the educational system. It is the only educational system that is directly involved in the whole life-long process of education from birth until death.

Impressive figures could be cited of the numbers of students in formal education who are taught by television. Impressive research findings of the effectiveness of learning by television could be referred to. Impressive examples of the use of television in both formal and continuing education could be given. But such citations, results and examples are not enough to resolve the crisis in the relations between the public television system and the American educational system.[22]

The withdrawal of support, actual or probable, by financially-strapped schools threatens the public television system.[23] Instructional television is its core. It provides the basic support for perhaps three-fourths of the stations. It provides nearly half of its programming. Without persuasive evidence that the public television system is increasingly valuable to formal education, some of its supporters in school boards, state legislatures and Congress will withdraw or withhold their support. But such evidence will not be available unless the educators use instructional television to do what it can do best to free the teachers to do what they can do best.

The withering or breaking of relationships between the public television system and the public school system is more threatening to the television system at the moment, because it is more dependent upon the schools than the schools are upon it. But in the not-so-long run, the deterioration of the relationship would be a grave loss to the public educational system too, and to the American people—a loss in opportunities not seized and developed.

In this crisis the task for the public television system in its educational role is to hold on and advance.

Testifying before the House General Subcommittee on Education, John W. Macy, Jr., President of the Corporation for Public Broadcasting, outlined some proposals for cooperative action:

"What is needed is a dramatic example of how the techniques of television—not merely a television camera trained on one instructor—can help the teacher in the classroom reach the students with lessons of importance. . . .

"If we provide an opportunity for television communicators

and educators to approach an education problem together, I am certain that the proper techniques would be found to match the medium and the message. . . .

"The subject matter for this project could be chosen by the Office of Education or the Department of Labor or any of the groups representing local school officials. The aim would be to pick a subject of national concern, a subject of vital interest to a substantial number of Americans.

"An example of the type of subject that might be selected would be remedial reading, or high school equivalency training for returning veterans. . . .

"Because of the great difficulties inherent in the local autonomy of our elementary and secondary education systems, it might be preferable to begin with some project in adult or continuing education." [24]

"If such a series as I propose . . . had one-tenth the impact on the nation as 'Sesame Street,' it could convince educators, school board members and Congress that television, properly used, can be the most effective tool for mass education yet devised," he added.

The public television system cannot intrude into instructional television at any level—national, state or local. But at all levels it can act as a "catalytic agent" in helping remove the blocks to the full use of the medium in both formal and continuing education. If these blocks are removed, a central instrument for education will not be lost. It will, instead, develop into a much wider facility—a national system of community-wide centers of communication and education, transmitting in many ways, processing data as well as programs, used cooperatively by many institutions and agencies. (This concept will be considered in later chapters.)

10. *To entertain*

Two meanings of "to entertain" (to hold attention agreeably) diverge. One is to divert and amuse trivially, the other is to play the host (a guest or an idea is entertained).

The public television system should not try to compete with

commercial television in mass entertainment that is merely
diverting and amusing. But to play host to a variety of publics
respectful of their many interests *is* a function and programming
goal appropriate for the public television system.

Public television cannot serve the whole variety of interests
(as wide as life), but it can serve many that commercial television neglects because the audience is deemed too small. We
need to refer to only a few that the British Broadcasting Corporation has served and developed over the years and that
many of the American stations are serving and developing:
interests such as natural history, archeology, astronomy, minor
sports and (in the United States) sports with a local flavor. [25]

Beyond the services to specialized interests, a function and a
goal for public television should be entertainment in its own
right — to give delight and joy and laughter, to move to tears
and to the "thoughts that do often lie too deep for tears," to
evoke wonder at the miracle that is everything, every one,
every day.

> *Trees are wooden monsters with color-changing hair.*
> *A cloud is the top of a person you don't know is there,*
> *A light bulb is an eyeball staring at the floor,*
> *A doorknob is an animal living on a door.*
> *If you believe in these silly things,*
> *Please call me up. My number is three dings.* [26]

Too zealous an intent to entertain can lead to the falsification
of what should be presented as unadorned as possible. Some of
the commercial newscasts are "Ho-ho-ho and here's the news" or
"the news—with a dish of dirt." One of the most able newspaper
TV critics in the United States, conditioned by "Perry Mason,"
found himself hoping for some "fireworks" while watching
"Trial—The City and County of Denver vs. Loren B. Watson."
In instructional television, "The proof of the academic pudding
is the learning, not the viewing; behavior, not 'circulation'." [27]

While no program should pander to interests, all programs
should be as interesting as possible as agreeably as possible.

Richard Hull, director of WOSU-TV, Columbus, rejects be-

lief in what he calls the Galahad Energy Law ("My strength is
as the strength of ten because my heart is pure") :

". . . This belief overlooks certain considerations e.g., the good
knight wore armor, he had a sword, and presumably ate large
quantities of protein to maintain his initial strength. When he
set forth to do deeds of valor and virtue, he was physically
equipped in much the same manner as a 'bad knight' and his
techniques in battle probably did not differ greatly from that of
his various opponents. His motivations, however, were quite
different and his goals were praiseworthy." [28]

Conclusions

From these statements of station functions and programming
goals there emerges a conception of the role of public television
requiring much more active participation by the people than
the conceptions in either the British Report of the Committee on
Broadcasting or the Report of the Carnegie Commission on Educational Television. The purpose is to enlist and employ the
widest range of energies and talents, not just for television, but
for the governance of our society. "Programming must tap the
intelligence within the city." "Public broadcasting should serve
as an active agent of change engaged in the recruitment of
people and talent in an adjustment of this society." "We need
education for potency . . . that's what we need very much
for television to give us. It should be called liberational, not
educational, television." [29]

Several consequences follow from the participatory role of
television for public purposes. One is that such television is
dangerous. Not one of the functions or goals identified in this
chapter is "safe." All are "hot." All are essential, all are vital,
and therefore all are controversial, because controversy is the
stuff that life is made of.

Another consequence is that several notions need to be re-
defined in order to be appropriate to the active role of the people in the public television system. "Professionalism" is required,
yes; but an element of the appropriate kind of professionalism

is the ability to elicit and employ the energies and talents of the people. "Excellence" should be the goal, yes; but excellence should be measured, not by "show-biz" standards, but by those that fit an instrument used by the people to further their serious private and public objectives.

The public television system—nationally and locally—cannot at any one time perform all the functions and seek all the goals that have identified. They are too many and too large, and, even so, they are multiplying and expanding. The public television system, nationally and locally, must set priorities and give emphases according to place and time and resources, and according to judgments of needs and opportunities.

It is good to have "so much to do, so little time." The public television system can try one thing after another. It can discard what does not work. It can cheerfully assign to the commercial media or to other agencies what they will take over. Then it can turn to new tasks and possibilities. It can build up a huge backlog of things it ought to do, would like to do, but cannot do because its financial resources or technical capabilities are limited. Then, when greater resources and capabilities come along, it will be ready to make use of them.

Some words of G. E. Bair, Director of Educational Television, the University of North Carolina, can be used to summarize this chapter:

"If public television is defined not as 'what is seen on the television screen' but what happens because television programs were seen on the screen, then the task of programming is put into proper perspective. Such a perspective makes inconsequential the arbitrary distinctions between 'instructional,' 'educational,' and 'public' broadcasting which have haunted us so long. Such a perspective also would insure that all the steps of programming are directed at an end which is understood at the beginning and which shapes all of the decisions along the way. . . .

". . . Programming is a process which begins with the ascertaining of a need in a potential audience which can be reached out to by television. There follows then the steps of sorting out priorities and objectives, the production of programs, the scheduling and dissemination of those programs, and hopefully the evaluation of the effectiveness of those programs, not in terms of numbers reached but in terms of the extent to which the objectives undertaken by the process were fulfilled." [30]

Those words also introduce the next chapter, which is about audiences.

1. *Public Television: A Program for Action*, p. 29.

2. In formulating these statements, the author consulted reports of many conferences and studies (some of which he took part in), beginning with the Allerton House Conference of 1949 and continuing through the Educational Television Stations Conference on Programming Goals in December 1969. He tried to catch what seemed a remarkably consistent development and a remarkably large consensus. The functions and goals could be (and have been) stated in different ways. No matter how stated, they always overlap and interrelate; the point is that the broadcasters and other knowledgeable persons identify a wide range of vital services to be provided to the community and of goals to be sought in programming. The illustrations, all taken from television, will be few and terse; others, perhaps better, could be cited; the point is that much is being done, locally, regionally and nationally, to try to provide those vital services.

3. For other cogent analyses of news and public affairs on television, see Harry J. Skornia, *Television and the News: A Critical Appraisal* (Palo Alto, California: Pacific Books Publishers, 1968), and Herbert J. Gans, "How Well *Does* TV Present the News?" *The New York Times Magazine*, January 11, 1970.

4. For a preview of possibilities that is at the same time expert scientifically and imaginative socially, see "Televistas: Looking Ahead Through Side Windows," by J. C. R. Licklider, a supplementary paper in *Public Television: A Program for Action*, pp. 201-25.

5. Television coverage of the courts was one of the subjects examined by "The Advocates" early in 1970. In his *Television and the News: A Critical Appraisal*, Harry J. Skornia sets up nine possible rules to govern broadcasting in the courts, rules that would serve both the right to a fair trial and freedom of the press.

6. This program proved to be "too hot to handle" for the Canadian Broadcasting Corporation and also for several members of the Canadian government.

7. *Transcript of Proceedings, Kettering Conference on Public Television Programming* (Dayton, Ohio: Charles F. Kettering Foundation, 1969) p. 40.

8. The "self-test" type of program, of course, has potentialities going beyond consumer-information programs to include many other kinds designed to engage active audience participation.

9. Louis Adamie, *A Nation of Nations* (New York: Harper & Brothers, 1945), pp. 6 to 13.

10. *A Nation of Nations*, p. 13.

11. Hearings before the Subcommittee on Communications, Ninety-First Congress, First Session, on S. 1242, p. 148. The Broadcasting Foundation of America promotes the exchange of taped radio programs between the United States and other nations. Although this book emphasizes television, the enormous advantages of radio and radio tape for promoting understanding between peoples should be noted.

12. Peter Adler, who has done more directing of opera for television in the United States than any other person, has commented: "The best hope for the development of a new audience for opera among young people is to develop a species of anti-opera. To reach young people with opera, we not only have to rid opera of its gaudy trappings, which the kids merely laugh at, but we also have to help in the creation of new works that speak directly to them."

13. In October 1970 the National Broadcasting Company network broadcast an hour-long compression of the series. It was in effect a promotion of the complete series to be presented beginning the next month by Public Broadcasting Service. The full commercial rate for the NBC broadcast was paid by the Xerox Corporation. This use of commercial television, underwritten by an industry, to promote public television programming is a remarkable instance of public service by a private corporation. The Xerox Corporation is underwriting the cost of importing the series over PBS.

Kenneth Clark (now Lord Clark), the series' "author" and commentator, regrets the "limitations imposed on me by the medium." He writes: "A line of argument determined almost entirely by visual evidence does not make for logic or completeness; and in the programmes it led to a number of omissions of which I am ashamed. Even the most rapid survey of civilisation should have said more than I have done about law and philosophy. I could not think of any way of making them visually interesting. This defect is particularly serious in my treatment of Germany. I talk a lot about Bavarian Rococco and hardly mention Kant and Hegel. Goethe, who should have been one of the chief heroes of the series, makes only a brief appearance, and the German romantics are left out altogether . . ."

In an article citing the above quotation, Robin Day, who regularly introduces "Panorama," the BBC's leading public affairs program, asks: "What does this lead to in the practice of television journalism? It means that TV can cover a riot, a war, a revolution, an assassination, more vividly than any newspaper. It also means that television tends to give much less impressive treatment of the reasons behind those events. In the case of events or issues which do not have convenient visual existence, television tends to treat them inadequately. Take a key issue such as the political implications for Britain of signing the Treaty of Rome. This is hard to deal with on television except by what TV professionals tend to regard as a second-hand and second-class way—by people discussing it. Television men have a revealing phrase for this. They do not call it 'argument' or 'the exchange of ideas'; they call it 'talking heads.' In that contemptuous phrase, the image merchants of the electronic age dismiss the one characteristic of man that elevates him above the beast, the power to conceive and communicate rational thought. Man's supreme gift is seen in terms of what the eye sees on that wretched little screen: 'a talking head'."—"Troubled Reflections of a TV Journalist." *Encounter*, May 1970.

14. *Proceedings,* p. 95.

15. *The Arts and the Poor,* p. 19.

16. *Inside Media*, Vol. 1, No. 1, published in New York City, appeared in March 1970, just in time for the first convention held by the publishers of the *Chicago Journalism Review.*

17. Edgar Dale's *How to Appreciate Motion Pictures*, a manual of motion-picture criticism prepared for high school students, is old and out of print. So is his *How to Read a Newspaper*. (He is writing a new book on the latter subject.)

18. "Louis Forsdale, professor of English at Columbia University's Teachers College, has spoken of the need for teachers to raise the level of literacy in the new media, as well as in print. He suggests that television be studied as a medium, and not just as an audio-visual tool, and notes that in Scandinavia schools are required to give at least one hour's instruction per week about film and/or television. He recently said, 'We study literature, not to create professional writers—we study music, not to create professional musicians. And we should study television, not to create television professionals, but to raise our students up the ladder of literacy in this new medium.' "—Roy Danish, in a talk, "The Shaping of the Television Medium," given at the Annual Convention of the Speech Association of America, December 1965.

19. Quoted in *To Improve Learning:* A Report by the Commission on Instructional Technology, p. 104.

20. "The Learning Force," pp. 3-4.

21. Television's "real strength is that it can communicate primary human experience, defying time and distance. More than that it *is* primary human experience . . . It would seem that the greatest service television can render, both in the classroom and for home viewing, lies in giving access to experience."—Henry C. Alter, *Of Messages and Media* (Boston: Center for the Study of Liberal Education at Boston University, 1968), pp. 5-6.

22. The most impressive example of what television can do in the elementary and secondary schools is the system in American Samoa, previously referred to. The success there encouraged the governments of the Ivory Coast and France; three United Nations agencies (UNESCO, the UN Children's Fund, and the UN Development Program) and the World Bank to join forces in setting up in the Ivory Coast Africa's first nation-wide classroom television system. However, the experience in the American Samoa has had no discernible influence upon the American educational system.

23. For example, the first statewide educational television network in the country was the first to be scrapped. Delaware's network died when the General Assembly ended its 1970 session on June 30 without providing the funds needed to telecast educational programs to the classrooms. Those close to the situation attributed the death of the five-year-old network less to a conscious decision by the state legislators than to effective criticism by legislators who sought to alter, rather than eliminate, the network's function and the state's tight financial position. Governor Russell W. Peterson said that

the statewide system could be converted to one of local control. It was not a "network" in the sense that programs originated from different points, but classroom teachers were able to choose from among programs on three channels. Some schools also had facilities for recording programs for use later. See "Delaware Drops Educational TV," *New York Times, July 5,* 1970.

24. The testimony was given December 18, 1969.

25. "Sports is a very strong cultural force, and a sociological tool, too. . . . . Sports is a universal talk; it's a universal appeal. Men, women, age groups, color—these are all brought together by a fundamental interest in sports. The interest in sports is also related to physical fitness, because none of the things we are talking about here are going to be of any value at all unless they are related to some healthy body. . . . you should not dismiss sports as a mindless activity, because there is a potential that should be tapped, not only for the enlargement of your audiences, but because sports is a very real experience for mankind, an enrichment for the audiences that you seek to serve."— William Reed, Commissioner, Big Ten Athletic Conference, at the Kettering Conference on Public Television Programming (*Proceedings,* pp. 113-114). A good example was the two-day coverage by WGHB-TV, Boston, of the U.S. Professional Tennis Championship, held in Brookline, Massachusetts, in August 1970. The program was carried over the Eastern Educational Television network. The station had a reporter who was independent of the participants in the sports and was thus able to ask some probing questions into the economics that underlie most sports, even many amateur sports.

26. A poem by 11-year-old Lorraine Adel, in *Anthology,* selected by the Creativity Research Center at Fordham University from writings by students in the fourth, fifth and sixth grades in public and private schools in metropolitan New York City. See "Child Poets Reveal Candid Visions of the World They See." The New York Times, September 4, 1969.

27. *Television in Instruction: What Is Possible,* pp. 22-23.

28. "A Review of Some Problems in Educational Television," October 1954, p. 12. Hull was then director of Stations WOI-AM-FM-TV, Iowa State College, the first university to enter the field of television. It did so on a commercial license.

29. These remarks are quoted from the *Proceedings* of the *Kettering Conference on Public Television Programming.*

30. From a letter to the author, October 30, 1969.

VI

THE MAKING OF CONSTITUENCIES

The objective of public television is not to agitate the air waves with emissions of high intent. It is not merely to be viewed by large numbers of people. Its objective is to make a significant difference in the lives of the people who watch its programs—significant in *their* estimates and useful for *their* purposes.

The justification of public television is broadcasting that serves the people's interests, rather than the interests of broadcasters who sell time and sponsors who sell goods or services. But a broadcasting service is (and should be) judged, not by its statements of functions and goals but by its programming service. The people do not care much whether the programs they watch are by CBS or NBC or ABC or by an independent station. Nor do they care much whether the programs are by public or commercial broadcasting. Public television must serve the people well.

"Audiences" is not a good word for those who receive public broadcasting when it is conceived (in the words of G. E. Bair previously quoted) "not as what is seen on the screen, but as what happens because television programs were seen on the screen." Better words are "constituencies" or "clienteles" because they imply that those served make use of the service and support the service they use. Any doctor, lawyer or politician could attest that clienteles, or constituencies, are made, not born—made and constantly maintained.

To be the people's instrument, television for public purposes must be "independent." What does that mean? The federal regulatory agencies, such as the Federal Communications Commission, are supposed to be "independent." But the other side of the coin of independence is political isolation. A main reason why these agencies have lost sight of the public interest is that, lacking any other clientele or constituency, they have leaned on the regulated industry officials for support. To be strong and free enough to serve the public interest, public television must develop constituencies that will give it strong support—financial support, of course, but other kinds as well: political, social, intellectual, and moral.[1]

Such support cannot be based on a misty belief that public television is "good for the society," or "good for the other fellow." It must be based on self-interest that is at the same time solid and enlightened. Freedom is defended and advanced when self-interest and basic principles *are seen* to coincide. The task of public broadcasting is to demonstrate that freedom of broadcasting coincides with the interests of the various minorities that make up the American society and with the good of that society as a whole.

What are the prospects that it can perform this task?

The Viewing of Television

Before inspecting some recent studies of the audiences that watch public television, let us sketch the context in broad strokes.[2]

The mass media are limited agents for social change and only one element among many others. With television (as with the other mass media and other activities) people are reluctant to expose themselves to what they do not want to receive and are likely to expose themselves to what they already favor.

The television-viewing habits of the American people have been stable for about a decade; that is, they are hard to change. Ownership of sets in households is nearly 100%. The watching of television is approaching the natural limits set by the fact that people must, or want to, do things other than watch television. Commercial "prime-time" viewing has been stable for years; overall viewing slowly increases, with more viewing during other hours. When stations in a community broadcast more hours of the day, viewing increases, but when more stations enter a market, the audiences are shared.[3]

"Specials" will alter audiences, but the previous patterns of viewing and non-viewing are quickly—all too quickly—resumed.

With the exceptions of those watching a few "specials" (like the flights of Apollos 11 and 13), *all* television audiences are minority audiences. Even the 60% of the sets turned on in regular "prime time" is divided among the three networks, the independent commercial stations and now the public stations.

In the main, the American people approve of commercial television. It is their choice among media. They criticize it on various counts, some of which are contradictory. But the percentages rating its performances as "excellent or good" are at least as high as the percentages making the same ratings for newspapers, schools and local government.

People do not always practice what they preach about television. They may say, "There ought to be more of x or y" (whether education or entertainment), yet not watch more when it is available. They may say, "There ought to be less of x or y" (triviality, brutality, sex, etc.), yet continue to watch what they say they condemn. They may say, "X or y is harmful," yet not have the slightest idea what it is all about.[4]

Television programs do not always reach the audiences they aim at. For example, the series "Young People's Concert," conducted by Leonard Bernstein, apparently reaches audiences that are mostly adult. "There are almost twice as many viewers of the show who are 50 years of age or older as there are viewers under 18."[5]

Television viewing is strongly influenced by the stage of the life-cycle a person or a family is in. Homes with children under six tend to watch more, homes with children from six to seventeen tend to watch less, teenagers watch least, old people watch most.

People with higher education levels tend to watch commercial television somewhat less than those with less education; this is apparently because they are more involved in other activities or with other media.

Viewers of educational television are also viewers of commercial television.

"There is little evidence that ETV viewers are 'refugees' from commercial television, althought about one fifth of them mention absence of commercials as one of the things they like best about ETV. Rather, they view a considerable amount of commercial television—both informational and recreational material. They come to ETV for *more* of the kinds of program they don't find enough of elsewhere, for a *different kind* of programming (e.g., intensive analysis of public affairs, programs on local problems) than they readily find elsewhere in the fields of their greater interests, and for *topics of interest for special audiences,* which other television cannot so readily provide.

"They are highly selective in the choice of programs. They go to the ETV channel typically for a program they have pre-chosen, rather than turning the station on and letting it play. They are tough critics of programs."[6]

With this transition, let us now look at some of the most recent and extensive studies of the audiences of public television.

The Viewing of Public Television

In 1969, after regular interconnections had been established for the educational stations and after the Corporation for Public Broadcasting had been operating for more than a year, several studies were made using interviews, by phone and in person, that for the first time gave some kind of picture of the audiences for public television in its new stage as a national system. Both the making and the interpretation of surveys are tricky businesses. Even to the untrained eye the several studies reported below vary in objectives, methods and quality. But they are what is available to study, and they are materials with which more extensive and careful surveys later can be compared. At the very least they refute the "image" of public television as being merely an added advantage for an already advantaged elite.

In October 1969 Louis Harris and Associates, Inc., conducted a national study of the reach of public television and the demographic characteristics of its viewers. They found that 74% of the American households were in range of a public television signal (39% VHF and 35% UHF) but that (because of UHF

handicaps) only 59% of the households could receive useable
signals from public television stations. With this 59% as the
base, 51% of the households had watched public television during the previous six months and 28% during the previous week.
With this same base, the percentages of those who had watched
during the previous six months ranged from 40 in the South to
64 in the Midwest; from 36 in rural areas to 57 in cities.

Still with 59 as the base, the figures of those who had watched
during the previous six months according to age brackets were:
51%—16 to 20 years; 55%—21 to 29 years; 51%—30 to 49 years;
and 48%—50 and over. The percentages for women and men
were about the same. The percentage for blacks was 56 and for
whites 53. Viewing rose with educational levels: 41%—8th grade
or some high school; 50%—high school graduate; and 61%— college. It rose with income levels also: 38% under $5,000; 47%—
$5,000 to $9,999; and 61%—$10,000 and over. The report ob-
served, "Other studies have shown that viewing of commercial
television is lower for the college educated than for those with
less education. At least in relative terms, public television has
reversed this pattern."

The Harris survey found that viewers of public television are
selective, with a high proportion of them tuning in to a specific
program they had known about beforehand.

The viewers split evenly on whether the public has special obligations to support non-commercial television: 40% said yes,
41% said no, 19% was not sure.

In summary, the Harris survey found that 45,000,000 people
in 15,000,000 households had watched public television over a
six-month period, and 24,000,000 in a one-week period; 51% of
the viewers had gone to college; one-third of them had less than
high school education; one-fourth earned $5,000 or less per year.

A Study of Seven Programs in Eight Cities

During late December 1969 Q.E.D. Research, Inc., studied
viewers of seven public television programs in eight cities.[7] The
results indicated that approximately 8,500,000 households, or

55% of the total, in the eight cities had watched public television during the previous six months; of the 55% 65% had watched during the week previous to the survey; an additional 23% had watched within the previous four weeks.

Public television households as a proportion of total households in the eight cities ranged from 37% in Los Angeles (where the public station is UHF and there are eleven other stations) to 78% in Boston. By income, the viewers of public television in the eight cities divided as follows: 12%—$5,000 or less; 27%—$5,000 to $10,000; 27%—$10,000 to $15,000; and 23%—over $15,000. By education, the grouping was 22%—some high school or less; 33%—high school graduate; 21%—some college; and 24%—college graduate or more.

Of the public television viewers polled in the eight cities, 48% thought that the public has a special obligation to help support non-commercial TV, 27% thought it does not, and 25% had no opinion.

"Sesame Street"

Of the public television-viewer households in the eight cities, 27% had children under six years of age; the Q.E.D. survey indicated that 78% of the households in this category had watched "Sesame Street." Nearly 800,000 viewers in the 2,300,000 households in this category had not watched public television before the debut of "Sesame Street."

Earlier surveys indicated that nationally "Sesame Street" reached about 6,000,000 children in 2,000,000 homes, day-care centers and nursery schools during the second week of its broadcasting (November 7, 1969).

A study made by Daniel Yankelovich, Inc., indicated that 90% of the children between two and five years of age who spent their days at home in Bedford-Styvesant, a ghetto area of New York City, had seen the program on a fairly regular basis. Sixty percent of them saw it one or more times daily. Reaching children in the ghettos has been a chief goal of the programmers of "Sesame Street."

"Newsroom" in San Francisco

In July 1969 Toklas Research, Inc., conducted interviews in five counties in the Bay Area concerning the viewing of and responses to "Newsroom," an hour-long week-nightly telecast of informal reports and discussions by the newsmen of KQED-TV, San Francisco.

Of the respondents, 49% said they had watched the station within the previous month, half of them several times a week. In San Francisco itself, 49% of the respondents said they had watched the station several times within the previous week.

Of those interviewed in the five-county area who said they had watched KQED, 48% said they had watched "Newsroom"— two-thirds at least once a week and two fifths almost nightly.

Of the total KQED-watchers interviewed, 23% were under 25 years of age and 17% earned between $5,000 and $10,000 a year. These populations and those with less than $5,000 were also the smallest percentages among the viewers of "Newsroom."

A little less than 10% of those who said they had watched KQED had subscribed money to the station; 13% of the viewers of "Newsroom" had subscribed. Of the viewers of "Newsroom" who are also subscribers, 54% said they were willing to pay a higher membership fee to keep the program on the air, and 45% of the viewers of the program who were not subscribers said they would be willing to make a contribution to keep it on the air.

WCNY-TV, Syracuse, New York

Two studies were made in 1969 of the viewers of Channel 24 in Syracuse (the only UHF station in the area)—one during May by Warren and Serena Wade, of Wade Media Consultants; the other during September by Mary O. Young & Associates, Incorporated.

The Young study indicated that 39.6% of the respondents' sets could not receive UHF. The main reason for not watching WCNY given by those who could receive a UHF signal was poor reception. This reason was given by a higher percentage of the black UHF viewers (45.8) than of the white UHF viewers (25.7). Nevertheless, the Young study indicated that 70.5% of the potential UHF viewers had watched WCNY; 15.5% stated they watched it daily. The Wade survey indicated that a larger percentage of blacks than of whites viewed Channel 24 and that blacks viewed some programs more frequently than whites did.

Both studies found that the Channel 24 audience was diverse. In the Young study, the white viewers described themselves as follows: 13.8%—professionals or executives; 9.6%—managers, officials or proprietors; 55.5%—blue collar workers; 12.5%—retired or widowed; and the rest as laborers, farmers or unemployed. In the same study the black viewers described themselves: 5.7% —professionals or executives; 2.3%—managers, officials or proprietors; 56.6%—blue-collar workers; 21.2%—unemployed; and the rest as laborers, retired or widowed. According to the Wade study, those whose education-level was high school or less made up 63% of the total viewers.

The Young survey catalogued the proportions of viewers according to age as follows: 7.5%—under 25; 22.5%—25-34; 27.6% —35-44 (with a substantially higher percentage of blacks in the last two age brackets); 30%—45 to 64; and 10.6%—65 or more (with a substantially higher percentage of whites in the last two groups).

WCNY broadcasts both its own Afro-American magazine-format program, "Black on Black," and the NET "Black Journal." The Young survey found that both white and black viewers in Syracuse much preferred the locally produced program to the network program.

Both white and black respondents in the Young survey favored greater racial integration in Channel 24's programming format, although 32% of the blacks stated a preference for separate black programming. However, Thomas Petry, then President of WCNY, commented: "...there is a large segment of the white community which appears to be unaffected by programming for and about the black community."

"The Numbers Game?"

Before considering what these findings mean, we should ask,
Are not such surveys just the public broadcasting system's way
of playing "the numbers game" to make it look good, just as the
commercial networks and stations pick the ways that flatter
them? Of course the interview method and all other methods
have limitations, but the question is deeper: What is the justification of counting viewing within the past six months, or one
month, or week?

The answer to that question lies in the public broadcasting
system's purpose to give people a choice of a kind of programming, alternative to the commercial kind, that they can use for
their own ends. When critical selectivity and active use are the
goals, instead of reflexive viewing habits and passive acceptance, then ways of audience research appropriate to those goals
must be devised—ways different from the how-many-sets-are-
turned-on-now or what-program-are-you-watching-now technique. The surveys cited above are steps toward devising techniques appropriate for studying the audiences of public television.
For example, before the Yankelovich survey in Bedford-Styvesant, who ever studied a ghetto area carefully to find out how
many children there were watching an educational program?

The logic of quantity, of mass, of the big-numbers game has
already led to insupportable conclusions in the United States:

The logic of the formal educational system has led to keeping
many young people in "preparation for life" until early middle
age (with consequent student unrest) and to the neglect of alternative ways of learning and of relating living to learning. In
one of the most careful studies made of the total American
"learning force" (all those engaged in systematic learning),
Stanley Moses estimated that in 1970 the number of adults engaged in systematic educational activities outside the traditional
educational system would slightly exceed the number of persons
enrolled in the traditional educational system, from kindergarten
through advanced studies.[5] Yet information on the adult education activities remains scant, unreliable and contradictory. The

consequence is that the institutions and activities outside the traditional educational system are ignored in educational planning and policy-making and are slighted in the allocation of resources.

In exact parallel, the logic of the commercial television has led to the passive diversion of tens of millions of people day after day to the neglect of pressing social problems. The consequence is that a broadcasting system offering alternative programming for serious and active purposes must struggle even to survive. The parallel can be extended further. The students in continuing education spend less time per year, month, day, than do the students in the formal educational system. This fact does not mean that the learning is less. (Do credit hours earned by students who really do not want to be in school measure learning?) Nor does it mean that the learning in continuing education is not significant in the lives of the students and for the society. Certainly the fewer hours spend by smaller audiences watching serious television can be more significant in the lives of the people and for the society than the massive numbers of hours spent by masses of people being diverted by commercial television.

The absurdities of the mass-numbers game are becoming apparent because the "mass" is differentiating:

The next period of American history, it is clear, will belong to the minorities; they are affirming the right to many different ways of life, to a variety of "life styles," rather than a single overwhelming "American way of life." The number of voters who classify themselves as "independent" has grown steadily to a total of 30% in 1969. Education levels continually mount: The percentage of high school graduates rose from 61 in 1960 to 75 in 1969; the percentage of people who have completed four or more years of college increased from 11 in 1960 to 16 in 1969; tens of millions of adults are systematically continuing their education. Such trends are toward more selectivity, more demands for wider choice.

Many forces are making it harder for commercial television to win "the numbers game." *Ebony* magazine showed that

strength lies in diversification. *Look* magazine is focusing on the
top sixty metropolitan marketing areas. Several other magazines
have, or are planning, "demographic editions." The Federal
Communications Committee plans to prohibit commercial television stations from accepting more than three hours a night
of network programming, which *could* mean fewer mass audiences.[9] Nationally and locally, citizen groups are pressing for
better commercial television and are challenging the FCC's near-
automatic renewal of licenses. Even the presidents of the three
national commercial networks have agreed that a reform in
the interpretation of audience ratings is long overdue and that
publicity rivalry bruiting high ratings should be kept within
bounds.[10]

The possibility cannot be discounted that television viewers
will revolt against the increasing number and intensity of commercials. In fact considering everything, including technological
developments, the possibility cannot be discounted that the
audiences of commercial television will "fractionalize" (to use
the trade jargon) as the audiences of commercial radio have already done. The day may soon come when the audiences that
public television can build up and maintain will look larger than
they do now when compared to the audiences of commercial
television.

However, even the "fractionalizing" of the commercial television audiences (if it occurs) will not change the need for the
different purpose and the different kinds of programming that
are the justification of the public television system. The main
reason for surveying the audiences of public television is to give
the public television system more knowledge about the characteristics and needs of the various publics it can serve. But there
is also a politics of statistics. The popular "image" of the public
television audience as a small elite no longer reflects the
reality.

The reality is rapidly becoming larger and more diverse. The
use of true and favorable facts in the promotion of public television is a legitimate way to cultivate supportive constituencies.

Conclusions

The public television system should be oriented to its audiences and its communities. However, the quest for audiences should not determine the programming; rather, the objectives of the programs should determine the audiences sought. Unless a "target" audience is defined in a specific objective, the aim is "general," which means random. Concern for audiences should permeate a process that begins with an analysis of the characteristics and needs of publics, and ends with an evaluation of results to improve the process.

Public television should not seek large audiences for the sake of numbers. However, unless the system serves a significant proportion of the people and a wide range of kinds of people, it cannot maintain its claim to be a public instrument. The goal for public television should be to have programs appropriate for a wide range of specified minorities and to have each specified audience as large as possible. Together, public television's audiences should be, if not literally all the people, at least all kinds of people.

Public television should suffuse its concern to serve minorities and to reach special publics with an equal concern to stress commonalities and to strengthen a sense of community.

According to recent surveys, the public television system is now serving more people and more kinds of people than it previously served. However, it still has a long way to go.

In the cultivation of larger and more varied audiences and the attempt to make a significant difference in the lives of more people of all kinds, public television must struggle against powerful forces in the society. People select what they are already favorably disposed toward. The preponderant "image" of television is that its purpose is to divert. Television-viewing habits are hard to change. They are strongly influenced by the stage of life a person or a family is in. The more highly educated people—who, in the main, are also people with high incomes—are more active in their approach to social and political affairs, including the use of television for serious purposes.

The less highly educated people—who, in the main, are also
people with low incomes—are more passive in their approach to
social and political affairs, including the use of television for
serious purposes (except when their close interests are touched).
Public television can modify some of these forces. By understanding them, it can use some of them to its advantage. But
by itself it cannot change them fundamentally.

Public television is closer to the cultivation of larger and more
varied *audiences* than it is to the cultivation of supportive *constituencies*.

It labors under many handicaps. Some of these handicaps
(such as too few stations, too low antennas, too little power, too
little mobile equipment, etc.) can be overcome with more
money. But some of its handicaps can be overcome only with
more knowledge, better planning, wider experience and deeper
experimentations.

Public television is in only the primitive stages of understanding and being able to manage the processes and relationships necessary to build supportive constituencies. Some aspects
of that process and those relationships will be considered in the
next chapter.

1. "It's a very difficult thing, being a public broadcasting organization, with
a national responsibility, and at the same time not being part of the establishment and part of the official mouthpiece of the government of the day."
—Leonard Miall, British Broadcasting Corporation representative in the United
States, to the Kettering Conference on Public Television Programming (*Proceedings,* p. 65).

2. To cite references for all the points that follow would be tedious. Two
main sources are *A Ten-Year View of Public Attitudes Toward Television and
Other Mass Media 1959-63,* by Burns W. Roper (New York City: Television
Information Office, March 1969) and Chapter V, "The Audience: How It Uses
Television," by Herman W. Land Associates, Inc., *op. cit.* An extensive biblio-
grahpy follows that chapter.

3. Ater 1955 the British people were given a choice between the programs of
the British Broadcasting Corporation (which previously had a monopoly) and
the programs of the Independent Television Authority supported by advertising. The broadcasting schedule of the BBC was lengthened to equal the schedule for the new commercial system. The increase in the amount of viewing

was proportionate to the increase in the hours of broadcasting and then leveled off. The amount of viewing in the homes that could receive both public and commercial programs was the same as the amount in the BBC—only homes. "The British example is especially interesting because it shows what happened when the viewer had a chance to turn from a restricted diet rich in 'uplift' to one with increased amounts of lighter entertainment. Going from programs requiring concentration to those which require no effort is a 'downhill slide,' whereas it is an uphill effort to go from easy, light entertainment to serious, thought-requiring programs. Even under these presumably optimal conditions, the amount of television viewing did not increase." —*The Wired City*, p. 122.

4. See Gary A. Steiner, *The People Look at Television*, a report of a study at the Bureau of Applied Social Research of Columbia University (New York: Alfred A. Knopf, 1963).

5. *The Wired City*, p. 136, with reference to NBC research data.

6. Wilbur Schramm, *The Audiences of Educational Television: A Report to NET* (Institute for Communications Research, Stanford University, February 1967), pp. 2-3. Schramm's portrait was, in the main, confirmed by a nationwide study of viewers of educational television made for NET by the Research Department of McGraw-Hill Publications in January 1969. The director of the survey concluded: "The overwhelming impression received by poring over the thousands of questionnaires generated by this study is one of involvement. The ETV audience is a highly enthusiastic one with a highly proprietary interest in ETV and its success. ETV audiences appear to identify intensely with educational television programming. ETV viewers have an extremely positive attitude toward non-commercial television. ETV viewers could almost be said to make educational television a part of their lives."

7. The programs (in the order of the audiences they attracted) were "Washington Week in Review," "NET Journal," "Sesame Street," "World Press," "Forsyte Saga," "The Advocates" and "Book Beat." (On the ranking of "Sesame Street" it should be noted that only 27% of the public television viewer households had children under six years of age in the household.) The cities were Boston, New York, Washington, D.C., Chicago, Memphis, New Orleans, Dallas and Los Angeles.

8. Stanley Moses, "The Learning Force," pages 12 and 20. There is a large overlap between the students in formal and in continuing education, of course, and it is increasing.

9. On the other hand, such a policy, both in intent and in result, could mean, not fewer mass audiences but more programmers—that is, independent syndicators—"getting a crack at" mass audiences. Conceivably a syndicator could sell his programs in the top twenty-five markets and get a mass audience immediately.

10. Jack Gould, "Network Presidents Ask Less Stress on Ratings." *New York Times*, March 12, 1970.

VII

SHAPING THE FUTURE

Those who control and direct the public broadcasting system should deal with the realities of today in ways that take account of the potentialities of tomorrow. In electronic comunications, as in all other areas of life, the main question is whether human policies will direct technology (as much as possible) or technology will largely determine policies.

The realities of today are that in the technology it can use public broadcasting is at a serious disadvantage compared to commercial broadcasting, with which it must inevitably compete for attention, time and support.

In 1969 47% of ETV station antennas were significantly lower than their commercial-station counterparts; 82% were operating below authorized visual power; 51% had no color facilities; 80% could not originate live color programming.[1] Moreover, many public television stations lacked such elementary equipment as mobile units and equipment for recording, storing and retrieving programs.

Public radio is at an even greater disadvantage. Most of the stations are clustered about the metropolitan complexes along the two oceans and the Great Lakes, and most of the rest of the country is unserved. More than a third of the stations can reach only from two to five miles. The public radio stations have no adequate national interconnections (although a start has been made through National Public Radio). In 1967 about a third of the stations had annual budgets of less than $10,000; almost half, less than $25,000; about six-sevenths, less than $100,000. The situation probably had not changed much by 1971.

While they must cope with such harsh realities, those who control and direct public broadcasting should at the same time project their thinking ahead to changes that are bound to make pub-

136

lic broadcasting either obsolete or much more capable and flexible.

They must try to abandon distinctions between radio and television; distinctions, even, between broadcasting and other kinds of electronic communications. They must try to rise above concepts limited by the frameworks of institutions and facilities. Only two concepts are lkely to remain useful: one, that of the *function* of reaching people by electronic means; and, two, that of the *process* of electronic comunications.[2]

The *function* of reaching people will be made much more powerful, diverse and flexible by developments (already in their early stages) in wireless systems, such as satellite transmission, and in wired systems, such as cable transmission.

Developments in transmission will, of course, also affect the *process* of electronic communications. In addition, the process could be made much more precise, effective and flexible by developments in analysis (information computers) and remote control (cybernetic computers), and by developments in program production, storage distribution and playing back (such as aural-tape, video-tape, etc.).[3]

Let us try (as those who control and direct public broadcasting should do) to look at the process of electronic communications with "one eye on the pot" of today's realities and "the other up the chimney" of future potentialities.

The Process of Electronic Communications

The organized management of the electronic communications process has been described as involving several interrelating steps. It is worth our while to look at each step and then compare the realities of today with the potentialities of tomorrow.

Step 1—the formulation of objectives: The tasks are to analyze the characteristics and to diagnose the needs of audiences (actual or potential), and then to determine desired responses to specific efforts (program objectives).

Step 2—the designing of programs: The tasks are to identify and assess resources (talent, materials, facilities, channels, times, etc.) in the light of objective, and then to plan a program.

Step 3—the production: The task is to bring the program into being, either by assembly or creation, or both.

Step 4—the transmission/distribution: A program may be transmitted or transported. A station may be an originator of a program or an intermediate agency between the producer (such as NET) and the person who receives the program.

Step 5—the reception/playback: A person at the other end of the transmission may be the ultimate receiver or an intermediate agent to record the program and use it later (or both).

Step 6—the evaluation of results: The tasks are to measure the size and characteristics of the audience, to ascertain the uses made of the program, to determine the degree of success in attaining objectives, and to review the entire process for improvements in subsequent efforts.

At every step in this process, the present capabilities of public broadcasting are either crude or limited, compared to the potentialities that are developing. Present ways of analyzing audience characteristics are both crude and limited. Present resources for programming are limited. The skills necessary to bring together the media and programming objectives are separated. Most stations today can transmit only one program at a time. The uses that those who receive programs can make of them are limited. Present methods of evaluating results are primitive.

Developing technologies—conceived of as intellectual as well as physical tools—could open up every step of the process.

The developing technology of gathering, storing, retrieving and analyzing information could vastly expand and refine the ability to study the charateristics and needs of audiences, at one end of the process, and to evaluate the results of programs, at the other end.

The developing technology of recording, storing and retrieving programs could vastly expand available resources for the production of programs using assembly and also both for transmission and for reception.

The developing technology of transmission/distribution could give the public broadcasting system many more channels and ways of communication, for both immediate and later use. Stations could serve many more audiences and meet many more needs.

The developing technology of remote control could make much larger, more flexible and more precise the capabilities of both transmission/distribution and reception/playback. The greater capabilities of receiving and playing back could magnify the power and increase the flexibility of both the intermediate transmitters (such as local stations) and the intermediate receivers (such as school systems, individual schools, individual teachers, etc.). The tyrannies of the clock and of the mass audience could be overthrown.

Many more people and resources could be involved in every step of the process of electronic communication—from the study of audience characteristics and needs, through the setting of objectives, the design and production of the programs (in some cases), the scheduling, the promotion, the reception, the uses of the programs after reception, to the evaluation of results.

These developments could be useful to many institutions, organizations and agencies in addition to the public broadcasting system. They could be useful for many purposes in addition to public broadcasting. They could lead to the concept and the practice of education-communications as a total service, instead of separated services by television, radio, telephone, computers, etc.[4]

The coherent assemblage and integrated use of such an education-communications complex would be enormously expensive in total outlay and operation, even though a coherent complex would enable many users to do many things they now cannot do and even though it would be economical for specific purposes through the sharing of uses and times. (A parallel is that a coherent electrical-supply or water-supply system is enormously costly in total, but is economical for individual users.) Therefore, the committee of the NAEB concludes:

"... our institutions should engage with others in cooperative planning and development of broad-scale community, regional

and national facilities to serve the whole spectrum of socially
needful interests. From this kind of cooperation may well emerge
across the country a number of variant but complementary 'mul-
ti-systems' for providing a wealth of essential communications
services to all those who can benefit from them.

"There is a *caveat* to all this, however. Cooperation in an enterprise of such vast and historic dimension should constitute
rational negotiations between respectful peers. The greater good
cannot come from communications planning in which the public
and educational parties, with the high social priorities of their
many tasks, are kept in secondary or lesser roles simply out of
custom.... What is truly equitable is what best meets the demands of all the American people for a total communications
service. Past forms, traditions, and relationships must not in-
hibit us. We must innovate, as must all other partes." [5]

The recommendation foretells what *could* be. Without cooperative planning and development, what *will* be is a multiplicity
of incoherent facilities and efforts that cost just as much in total
but that do not provide a total service or maximum return. A
dispersion of facilities and efforts would do fewer things and do
each of them less well because it could not do the rest. The public broadcasting system could lose one function after another to
one agency after another. Its unique function could wither and
not be performed at all. The American people could lose the
benefits of a public broadcasting service; they could lose also the
potential benefits of a total education-communications service.

Such is the process of electronic communications. Such are the
alternative futures. Let us now follow some of the implications
for the policies of the public broadcasting system, of television in
particular. The counsel that follows is an attempt, not to give
formulas or prescriptions, but to state some basic principles.

*1. In its boards, staffs and advisory bodies, the public broad-
casting system should be fairly representative of the American
people.*

We have already been told all we need to know about the importance of having the media of mass communications represent

the American people fairly and the necessity, therefore, of having
the American people fairly represented *in* the mass media. With
the initial and follow-up reports of the National Advisory Commission on Civil Disorders; with the several reports of the National Commission on the Causes and Prevention of Violence, in
particular the recommendations of its Study Group on the Mass
Media; with surveys by such groups as the NAACP Legal Defense and Education Fund, the Office of Communications of the
United Church of Christ, and the Fordham University Conference on Equal Opportunities in Broadcasting; with the findings
(and sporadic actions) of the Federal Communications Commission and the Department of Justice; and so on and on—with all
these at hand, do we need more information?

No, we have enough information about the importance of having fair representation in the media of mass communications, and
enough, too, about the fact that fair representation *does not exist,* either in the media or in the institutions and agencies that
influence them. Reports proving this fact abound, for those who
want to find them, but expert surveys are not necessary: All one
needs to do is to review at random the boards and the staffs—
with attention to their *roles*—in the commercial networks and
stations, in the Federal Communications Commission, in the
foundations, and, yes, in the field of public broadcasting—the
Public Broadcasting Corporation, the old NET and new Educational Broadcasting Corporation, the individual stations, etc.
The American people are not fairly represented in the media of
mass communications in the United States, public or private, or
in the institutions and agencies, public and private, that influence
these media.

What would "fair representation" be? The question cannot be
answered with a formula. Minority groups in the United States
are many, overlapping, complex and diverse. Who is "representative of American Negroes/blacks? or of "Spanish-speaking
Americans"? or of the young? or of women? And so on. The application of any formula would not bring about programming
that is fair and sensitive. The question of fair representation
must be answered in practice, and that it is difficult, perhaps

impossible, to answer completely, cannot be accepted as an excuse for not trying.

To try to answer the questions in practice would be to work toward programming that is fair and sensitive. Fairness is a state of mind and heart, involving concern, insight, sympathy. But sensitivity requires something more, perhaps "empathy" is the word, that comes only from experience:

"Black and other minority people have suffered more, are more sensitive to social problems and injustices. Our leadership of America will come just as easily and naturally as has our leadership in American music. We know more about pollution, dope, abuses of power, not to mention white disregard for law and order. Consequently, we and other minorities in America are truly sensitized to the moral, spiritual, political, social and economic problems which would concern the leadership of a country. Our sensitivity not only develops from our recent history, but from our ancient history, which, despite present scholastic hypocrisy, goes back over ten thousand years. . ." [6]

Concern, insight, sympathy, empathy . . . Such qualities mean nothing until they are translated into the *sharing of power*. The sharing of power is the heart of the matter. It has always been the heart of the American experiment in government. To Jefferson's query, "If a person cannot be trusted to govern himself, how can he be trusted to govern others?" there is no answer. The sharing of empathy and power must be built into the corporate structure of the media of mass communications and the agencies that influence them. The consequences in programming would inevitably follow.

The public broadcasting system has not yet given the lead in the sharing of empathy and power that it is obligated to give. The obligations are legal and ethical. But, deeper than obligation is the *necessity for fair representation if the public broadcasting system is to perform its functions and achieve its objectives*. Without fair representation on boards, staffs and advisory groups, it will not be aware of needs and opportunities to serve; it will not be trusted by many groups; it will not be able to portray the American experience in all its strengths and resiliencies as well

as in its weaknesses and rigidites; it will not be able to attract
the talents and to liberate the vitalities of persons, volunteer and
professional; it will not be able to serve as a social as well as an
electronic medium; it will not be able to cultivate a broad base of
constituencies; it will not be able to *involve* various kinds of
Americans as serious, intelligent persons with broad civic concerns, in contrast to spokesmen for particular interests of race,
creed, color, sex or age.

Miss Jean Fairfax on May 14, 1970, put some questions to the
commercial broadcasting industry that, broadened to include
minorities in addition to black and adapted to the non-commercial situation, are sharp challenges to the public broadcasting
system at all levels:

"1. What steps are you taking now to identify those practices
of your management and your affiliated unions which act to pre-
vent the rapid mobility of blacks in your organization?

"2. What affirmative programs do you have to recruit, train
and upgrade blacks into positions where controlling decisions
about programming are made? What are you doing now which
will ensure the presence of black station managers, program direc-
tors, vice presidents and presidents of major networks with something faster than deliberate speed?

"3. What funds are you investing in black institutions to ensure a flow of blacks into your industry?

"Your industry cannot stop, direct or control the black revolution. This is not in your hands. You may be able to reduce
some of the causes of black rage. You may be able to present the
adversaries in the growing racial struggle as complex men and
women, who are honest and worthy opponents. You may be able
to reflect in your own industry the kind of society America must
become if it is not to fall apart. These decisions *are* in your
hands."[7]

2. *The public broadcasting system at all levels and in all ways
should create a climate hospitable to creative people.*

It should give talented people as much freedom as possible and protect them as much as possible from pressures and retaliations. The purpose of public broadcasting—to enlarge the freedom to express and the freedom to receive—coincides with its operational need for talent. The talent indispensable to high quality broadcasting will be attracted and retained most of all by freedom.

Freedom will attract many persons of unrecognized talents who will not compromise for money. It will attract many persons of recognized talent who will accept less money for fewer constraints.

A climate hospitable to creativity cannot be concocted by formula. However, some clues may lie in an analysis of the characteristics of a scientific environment that is most hospitable to the talents of researchers. The National Academy of Science reported to a House committee that five characteristics of the research environment facilitate the transfer of new scientific knowledge to useful application. Edited to fit public broadcasting, these characteristics are:

"a. Talented individuals are fully aware of and sympathetic to the principal goals of the organization, and their mission is defined in broad enough terms so that it retains its validity as circumstances and the state of the technology change.

"b. Talented individuals are willing to move between creation and production, and are willling also to change roles. Artificial barriers are kept at a minimum.

"c. The organization is quick to recognize new ideas and to fund work based on them up to the point where the feasibility and desirability of a larger commitment can be assessed.

"d. At each organization level, the creative individual has some freedom in deploying the resources at his disposal without extensive review of higher authority.

"e. There is full communication through all stages of the process, from original idea to ultimate program."[8]

3. *The public television system at all levels and in all ways*

should engage its operations in the operations of a wide spectrum of social forces and institutions.

It should engage in and be engaged by the activities of many people and groups. This is not counsel for good public relations. It states a basic principle whose implications drive to the heart of the justification for public television, which is to make a significant difference in the lives of the American people. That means helping them become more effectively active through knowledge and skill.

The task of public television is to make the process of programming an integral part of the processes by which people understand and manage their affairs. "Sesame Street" illustrates the point happily. It is not just a "television program." It is now an organic part of activities in millions of homes, nursery schools, day-care centers—indeed, the activities of all groups concerned with healthful growth in early childhood. It involves a wide range of the activities of other media, public agencies and voluntary organizations.

Each station function and programming goal entails participation by the people as individuals and through their various organizations and institutions. The role of public television is to act as "catalytic agent." Its role is to provide "education for potency." (This argument has been developed in Chapter Five and will be developed further in the next chapter.) Getting people to watch public television is only a means to getting them to use public television as an indispensable instrument in the conduct of their affairs.

People who use tags have identified many "gaps" in the American society, for example, the "generation gap." Is the gap between generations greater today than it has always been? The point can be argued, but that the world today is different from the world of all previous generations cannot be argued. It is a world of change so rapid that the "linear transmission" of learning from the older generation to the younger has lost much of its appropriateness. What we need (in Margaret Mead's phrase) is "lateral education"—learning by people of all ages from one another, all learning together how to cope with the flux that is

now the only constant. The best way to such learning—and also
the best way to bridge all the gaps—is for people to work together in the solution of their common problems. Insofar as public television facilitates common activities, it is stressing commonalities and strengthening a sense of community.

The Public Broadcasting Corporation has formed an Advisory
Committee of National Organizations, and most stations have
advisory groups of citizens. (Some of these helped organize the
televised town meetings held in twelve cities in conjunction with
the December 1969 White House Conference on Food, Nutrition
and Health.) Such are seeds—small seeds that have merely begun to sprout. But, like mustard seeds, they can become trees
"big enough for the birds to come and roost." Their growth
should be nurtured with care. However, the engagement that
matters most is not achieved through formal organization; it is
achieved in the day-to-day operations of the programming process.

At the risk of chopping words, let us note a limitation in the
concept of public television as a "catalyst." A catalyst causes
activities in other bodies or forces while itself remaining un-
changed. But public television will change. Its growth should be
directed away from being a broadcasting institution (whether a
system or a station) and toward becoming a public educational
communications agency.

4. *The public television system at all levels should define
"community" in ways that take account of both the complexity
and diversity of society and also its own developing potentiality
to serve more different kinds of communities.*

All agree that each public television station should be oriented
to its own community and that all other arrangements, national
or regional, should serve the local station. But what *is* a "community"?

A start toward answering that question is to recognize that
each community of locality is its own unique "mix" but that
there are many other kinds of communities. Some other kinds
are more signficant to their members than the de facto commu-

nity of geography. There are communities of common concerns and interests, of common origins and aspirations; there are communities of common problems or grievances; both of these kinds may be dispersed all over the country or even the world. The members of such communities may not be aware of their commonalities, much less be organized around them. A civilized person is consciously aware that he has membership in many overlapping communities, but, civilized or not, each of us is a member of more communities than he knows.

A striking trend in the world today is the development of senses of belonging to special communities that may have little or nothing to do with locality. A main reason for this development is the wider awareness promoted by the mass media. This trend has probably gone farthest in the United States, partly because here the influences of the mass media are most pervasive.

The immediate implication of these facts is that the public television stations should be aware of the many kinds of communities that the people in range of their signals belong to—communities not embraced by neighborhood. The stations should serve as many different kinds of communities as possible, with full appreciation of the complex and far-reaching web of relationships that make up the American society. The study of audience characteristics and needs is essential for such appreciation.

Technology sharply limits the number of different kinds of communities that public television can serve today. But new technologies will open up many new capabilities.

Within a city television could enable school administrators to achieve decentralization: "Television can enable ... administrative complexes to group their individual schools—or even classrooms—into numbers of different, operating 'districts,' each with its own special curricular patterns. Futhermore, because of the very nature of the electronically-facilitated cooperation which can be established between the elements of these new school units, they need not be geographically contiguous to function effectively." [*]

With satellites, the capabilities could extend to the national **community:**

"I am especially interested in the possibilities of developing school 'systems' that are not geographically common or contiguous, but are educationally related. For example, an inner-city school system could be 'established' electronically by providing special instructions to students whose skills and educational opportunities need particular attention. The same 'system' could involve a large number of inner-city school locations throughout the country." [10]

By means of cable or satellite transmission, or both, within a metropolitan area or within the whole country, the new kinds of school "systems" could include many kinds of special "populations" in addition to those of the inner-cities. They could include, for example, those persons in rural areas, those who are especially gifted in one way or another, those who have special needs or interests in languages other than English or in the learning of English as a second language. They could include students in high-school-equivalency or basic-adult-education programs, those in vocational or professional programs of continuing education, and so on. A "district" could be defined according to common problems or objectives, rather than geography. Since television can erase distinctions of place, the entire country could be made neighborhoods of special groups for special purposes.

The developing capabilities for television open up opportunities to serve special populations, not just in education, but also in all kinds of other activities. These capabilities could lead to a new kind of networking for special tasks and audiences—audiences that are nationwide but not national. The networking service could be for immediate and simultaneous transmission, or it could be for recording, reproducing, storing and distributing later to use in many flexible and adaptable ways.

The board committee of the National Association of Educational Broadcasters foresees new relationships between the national, regional and local educational broadcasting institutions:

"...In the past and still at present, there were distinct differences between programs prepared and circulated from these separate levels, not only in terms of quality and cost, but also with respect to the focus of their objectives and contents.

"We predict that these same distinctions between, say, network-originated programs and those done purely for local consumption will continue, with a special new emphasis made possible by adequate funding of the Corporation for Public Broadcasting. Nevertheless, we foresee that innovating technologies, and the policies surrounding them, may well lead to new kinds of 'national' and 'regional' programs which conform to the dominant, highly-specialized characteristics of what have heretofore been considered as 'local' efforts. This would result from: (1) our improved capacities to specify audience groups by demography, entry behaviors and social/personal deficits; (2) our enhanced abilities to accomplish practical program planning and production by geographically-dispersed persons and agencies; and (3) our strikingly increased capacity in program distribution and transmission to individuals and institutions. This kind of programming phenomenon would allow many separated and fragmentary local audience groups of common characteristics and needs to receive especially devised materials prepared and transmitted/distributed on a nation-wide or regional basis."[11]

Two of the basic principles are so closely related that they are stated together. They apply to fields so technical that only a few general comments follow them.

5. *The public broadcasting system should support and participate in research, experimentation, demonstration, development and application of new ideas and practices.*

6. *The public broadcasting system should support and provide opportunities for professional development.*

To become an instrument that the American people will use for their vital purposes, the public broadcasting system must be daring. It should try to convert uncertainties into well calculated risks wherever possible.

To influence and exploit the potentialities of technology, the system needs to look and feel ahead as far as possible.

To understand audience characteristics and needs and to evaluate results, the system needs new kinds of methods for research, analysis and evaluation.

To understand and use the process of electronic communications, the system needs new kinds of professionals—people who are at home in the fields of research, of audience analysis, of subject-matter specialities, of the media, of promotion, of evaluation, etc. Especially it needs people who can design and produce programs that relate the capabilities of the media to specified objectives for specified audiences.

Much of the research, experimentation and development significant for public broadcasting will be done by people in other fields; some of it must be done in cooperation with them. The same point applies to opportunities for professional training.

The developing technologies of electronic communications will enlarge opportunities for research, experimentation, demonstration and development. They will also enlarge opportunities for training new kinds of professionals.

A part of the new professionalism should be skills in eliciting and employing the talents and resources of participating public groups.

One purpose of the training should be to prepare an increasing number of people from minority groups for employment.

7. *The public broadcasting system should work out for itself an economic rationale based on a systematic approach using basic principles of management, administration, budgeting and analysis.*[12]

Public broadcasting is now achieving some effectiveness. It needs and is asking for large-scale continuing financial support from various sources for various purposes, but particularly from public sources for essential social services. It must understand why it should get this support, and it must be able to persuade those who could support it to do so.

The need for an economic rationale has nothing to do with the difference between commercial and non-commercial broadcasting. It is a basic need in all advanced societies, whether "Communist," "Socialist," "Capitalist" or what-have-you. It concerns decisions about the allocation of scarce resources for competing purposes and about the choice of alternative ways of achieving those purposes. In the American society all government agencies need economic rationales. So do all divisions or departments of other institutions—educational, commercial, etc.

Here are some of the questions that public broadcasters are asked and must be able to answer:

Why should there *be* a public broadcasting service in addition to the service of the commercial system?

If subsidized programming is necessary, why should the subsidy be through the public broadcasting system rather than through sponsorship on commercial broadcasting?[18] Or why not through subsidies directly to the sources of programs, such as orchestras, operas and universities, so they can use commercial broadcasting?

Cannot the results be better achieved by ways other than broadcasting—through pay TV, say, or print, or records, or tapes —with or without subsidy?

If public broadcasting is the best means, why television rather than radio? How much money should go to national agencies and how much to local stations? Which national agencies? Which local stations? On what grounds?

If subsidies are necessary, what sources should they come from, and why?

If public funds are necessary, what should be the sources, and why? If public taxation is the source, what is the appropriate theory of taxation—the general good, the ability to pay, benefits received? Which, therefore, is the appropriate kind of tax—general revenue, users tax, or what?

What broadcasting services are for what objectives? How long should support be continued? During a pilot project only? for a particular program or series? Indefinitely?

What are the specific objectives of particular efforts, and how can the results of those efforts be measured?

*   *   *   *

The public broadcasting system must be able to answer questions such as these—answer them convincingly and in a patterned way.

The economic rationale that the public broadcasting system needs cannot be just a "sales pitch." It must be a systematic approach using basic principles that will guide planning and execution. It must guide internal decisions concerning the use of resources ("Should we do this or that? How much should we allocate to audience analysis, how much to program design, how much to programming, how much to promotion, how much to evaluation?" etc.).

An economic rationale would require the hardest kind of rational thinking (in the economic sense) concerning basic purposes, alternative ways, all the steps of the communications process—particularly the setting of objectives and the evaluation of results.

An economic rationale would guide decisions to include or exclude, to continue or to drop, to set priorities and to give emphases.

An economic rationale would necessarily be complex. It should be adaptable to many situations and adaptive as circumstances change.

An economic rationale would necessarily contain tensions. For example, there is the need to be vital (and therefore controversial) in order to perform essential social functions; there is also the tendency to be inoffensive in order to win and hold support from certain sources.

The struggle between the urge to be vital (and therefore controversial) and the drag to be cautious (and therefore non-controversial) is more than an illustration of a tension within an economic rationale. It is an indicator of the *nucleus of the problem of the public broadcasting system:* Can the system get enough funds from enough sources sufficiently free and sufficiently assured so that the people who produce the problems and who make decisions about production and presentation can do the job that is the justification of having a public broadcasting system? We will return to this problem at the ends of the next two chapters.

An economic rationale would have to take into account "opportunity costs"—the cost of not doing X because the decision is to do Y. An important part of the argument why the American people in various ways should support public broadcasting is the "opportunity cost" to them if they do not have the essential services that only public broadcasting can provide. However, this argument must be persuasive, as specific as possible, and demonstrable by previous achievements.

"Accountability" is being required of all American institutions and operations. Demands for goods and services are infinite, resources are finite. Alternative ends and means are multiplying; many of them are competitive, some of them are mutually exclusive. The American people must set standards and priorities to guide choice.

Nicholas Johnson told the National Association of Educational Broadcasters, "You're committed to a particular technoloy, but your user is not." The American people are not. Congress is not. State legislatures are not. School boards are not. Foundations are not. Corporations are not. Voluntary organizations are not. The users and sources of support, actual or potential, are interested only in results. The test is, will they put public broadcasting into their budgets? Public broadcasting can prepare for that test, not by arguing that it is "good," but by arguing and proving that it is useful and effective.

Conclusions

If it is able convincingly to argue and demonstrate that it is useful and effective for many purposes (all of them specific, although some of them large), public broadcasting may get the financial support it needs to provide an adequate and sustained service.

If it proves itself indispensable in the activities of many individuals, groups, agencies, organizations and institutions, public broadcasting may get the social, political and moral support—the constituencies—it needs to be strong and free.

If it looks ahead clearly enough and plans well enough, public broadcasting may be able to exploit the advantages of the new technologies that are developing.

By having "so much to do, so little time," public broadcasting can be ready to use the new technologies. It can be ready persuasively to argue its case, with constituent support, for the adequate room on cables, satellites, data systems, remote control systems, etc., that it *must* have to perform its expanding mission.

In all these ways, public broadcasting could influence commercial broadcasting to give better service. The many audiences of public broadcasting are increasing. Some of the mass audiences of commercial television are likely to break up. The American people's demands for greater diversity and a wider range of choice in programming can be expected to increase with more experience and a constantly rising level of education.

In all these ways public broadcasting could be able to take part as a "respectful peer" in the cooperative planning and development of a total educational-communications service for the American people. Public broadcasting may even give the lead—for, after all, it is the only educational-communications system in direct touch with all levels and phases of education, the only one directly involved in the entire life-long process of education, the only one in direct touch with all levels of government.

Public broadcasting probably will lose some of its functions to cable transmission and gain some others through satellite transmission. Public broadcasting may change so much as to be unrecognizable in the "stations" as we know them today. Other institutions also may change so much as to be unrecognizable in the forms and procedures we are familiar with today. For example, in Philadelphia and Chicago there are experimental "schools without walls," which use the community as their learning environment. Vocational education is becoming related to life—with alternating rhythms of study and work; some of the alternating periods are half-days, some are months or even years in length. Wherever learners are, in place or time, public broadcasting can serve them.

Open broadcasting will probably remain the means of transmitting electronic signals that is most economical—most economical in initial outlay and continuous operation, and, what is more important, most economical for those who receive it. This advantage is especially great in all effort to expand educational and social opportunities for poor people.

The danger that electronic communications will lead to greater standardization and conformity can probably be avoided. Therefore the likelihood that satellite transmission will make local "stations" or "centers" obsolete is probably lessened. More likely, the proper uses of satellite transmission (in combination with the other means of transmission/distribution) will enrich and broaden the roles of "stations" or "centers" that are oriented to particular communities—with communities defined in ways that fit social realities. (The use of the telephone to call across town or even across the street has not gone down because one can dial long distance numbers. The use of the mails has not gone down because one can transmit messages electronically.)

American life could be made diverse by the ability to communicate simultaneously to populations separated by distance but related by common problems, needs or concerns. The sense of citizenship in a "nation of nations" could be strengthened.

The question is, will the policies of the public broadcasting system and of other systems be able to direct technological developments, or will technological developments largely determine their policies? That way of putting the question is useful because it calls attention to the great danger that technological developments will dominate policies. But the ability to direct technological developments can be overestimated, for two reasons: One is that developments in technology and their social consequences can be foreseen only dimly at best and often not at all. A second reason why present planning can control the uses of technology only within narrow limits is quite different: Developments in technology solve some problems, create other problems and change the nature of still other problems.

"It is in the nature of our scientific development," as William G. Harley has pointed out, "that the capacity to resolve a problem often reveals the problem. For example, to know that communication technology can link together educators involved in common tasks is to emphasize the common failing of trying to resolve many important educational issues on too small a scale— usually in the self-contained classroom. . . . It may seem gullible to accept the hardware in advance of the software, but the chances are we will end up resolving a different and broader problem than the one we start with." [14]

The author of those penetrating words follows their implications into fields broader than education: "Unlike any other available means, it [communication technology] can provide the central means for implementing an integrated approach to educational planning and development. In this context, radio and television, together with supporting electronic media, are seen not merely as a means for transmitting instructional materials, but rather as basic instruments for developing improved, comprehensive approaches to the management of solutions to social, economic and environmental problems." [15]

This line of thought projects our argument into the subject of the next chapter.

1. Testimony by William Harley, the President of the National Association of Educational Broadcasters, before the Subcommittee on Communications and Power of the Committee on Interstate and Foreign Commerce, House of Representatives, Ninety-First Congress, First Session, on H.R. 4214, H.R. 7737 and S. 1242, p. 93.

2. For ideas from this point through the following section on "process," the author acknowledges heavy indebtedness to the "Report of the NAEB Board Committee on Long-Range Planning," *Educational Broadcasting Review*, February 1970.

3. The allusions to technological developments are kept to a minimum and made general so as to avoid being lost in details, complexities and uncertainties. The gain in simplicity was paid for with a heavy cost—the omission of treatment for example, of cable television and videotape cartridges. Both of these vast continents will soon be explored in the 1970s. The Alfred P. Sloan Foundation in 1970 made a $500,000 grant to create a Commission on Cable TV. No comparable study had yet begun of the potentialities of the video-cartridge, making its entrance in the fall of 1970 with the mass-marketing of the CBS Electronic Video Recorder, with the Sony Corporation of America and RCA soon to follow and other corporations moving in the wings. The author

of this book, faced with the choice of making rough sketches that would have to be labeled "Terrae Incognitae" or passing them by, decided to sail past, with nothing more than the recognition that each by itself will probably change mass communications and individual habits in degrees comparable to the changes brought about by the introduction of open-broadcasting television, and that together they will probably change the "internal environment" of the American people beyond calculation.

4. "It is quite likely that special community — or state — agencies will eventually emerge to manage electronic distribution complexes which will offer access to a variety of transmission facilities. Under such a scheme, school systems, colleges, training centers and other educational agencies will have privileged use of appropriate audio, video and data channels. A concerted arrangement of this sort could mean an efficient, maximized exploitation of available spectrum and cable circuits. There are those who predict that existing organizations like ETV stations, Educational Media Centers and Regional Laboratories may serve as administrative nuclei around which these valuable transmission complexes might be formed. Embryonic developments of the sort are already 'in the works' in Cleveland, Appalachia, and northern Virginia. All this points up the oft-quoted fact that *one properly designed technical system can facilitate a number of different instructional and data systems,* thus greatly enriching investment returns."—*Television in Instruction: What Is Possible,* p. 24. The same paper (p. 18) makes a point about the integrated use of the media in instruction that is applicable to the integrated use of the media in the community: "It does many things and it does each of them better because it does all the rest."

5. "Report of the NAEB Board Committee on Long-Range Planning," pp. 28-20.

6. "100 Madison Avenues Will Be of No Help," by William Greaves, *New York Times,* August 9, 1970. Until he recently became an independent film and TV producer, Greaves was Executive Producer of "Black Journal."

7. Miss Fairfax, former dean of women at Tuskegee Institute, is director of the division of legal information and community service for the NAACP Legal Defense and Educational Fund. At the same meeting Ossie Davis told the broadcasting industry that blacks had arrived too late to share in the fruits of the radio, television and motion picture industries, but that they would be there with their demands for representation when the licenses for cable television are handed out by the Federal Communications Commission: "Cable TV is another ball game and we're not going to wait for others to give us a share." Mr. Davis, an actor and playwright, is co-chairman of the Full Opportunities Committee of the National Academy of Television Arts and Sciences.

8. See an editorial by Philip Abelson, *Science,* June 23, 1967, p. 1567.

9. *Television in Instruction: What Is Possible,* p. 18.

10. William G. Harley, "Educational Uses of Satellites in Developed and Less Developed Countries," NAEB 1969, p. 10.

11. "Report of the NAEB Board Committee on Long-Range Planning," pp. 18-19.

12. The source of all the ideas in this section is the transcript of remarks

by Commissioner Nicholas Johnson before the National Association of Education Broadcasters, Washington, D.C., November 20, 1968.

13. In April 1970 the AVCO Corporation, through the agency Greer, DuBois, ran full-page advertisements in fifty major newspapers and *Life* magazine, with the headline "If you have something important to tell America, we'll put you on national television to say it." The ad announced:

"Beginning in August this year we are turning over our television commercial time—time we'd ordinarily spend talking about our divisions, the products they make and the services they provide—turning it over to individual Americans like yourself.

"Americans who strike us as having something fresh and original to say to their countrymen.

"If you are chosen, we will send camera crews to wherever you live. We'll film you while you say what's on your mind, in your own words, in your own way. Then we'll put as many of you on TV as possible."

14. William G. Harley, "Educational Uses of Satellites in Developed and Less Developed Countries," p. 4.

15. *Ibid.* p. 8.

SERVING PRIORITIES

If those who allocate resources decide that "public broadcasting is something it would be good to support but the money is needed for more important purposes," then public broadcasting will remain on the level of subsistence. If they decide that it is useful in fulfilling those other purposes, then public broadcasting will share in the priority allocation of resources. It will share, not as a competing priority, but as an instrument in the other priorities. The decision one way or the other will turn partly on whether public broadcasting *really does* serve priorities effectively and partly on whether public broadcasters argue their case convincingly. The right points must be put in the right places at the right times and then be driven home by the "clout" of the right constituencies.

However, the case must be stated correctly. Beneath the familiar problem of marshaling support lie deeper questions: What *are* priorities? How must priorities be set in the American society if they are to be followed? How must they be acted upon if they are to be put into effect?

To set priorities means to compare items, then to rank them in order of precedence. Priorities imply, in one direction, values and attitudes that determine the criteria of choice. They imply, in the other direction, action programs to implement them. In a democracy the priorities must accurately reflect the values and attitudes of the people; the people must understand the reasons for and the details of the action programs and must take part in carrying them out.

Most "priorities" are reactions to, not anticipations of, problems. Most action programs try to put out fires instead of preventing them. "Priorities" burst upon the people like the "news" that didn't exist until the explosion. They are like headlines, without context or meaning. Slogans are substituted

for analysis; the promotion of slogans is substituted for understanding; words are substituted for deeds; "whipping up a storm"
is substituted for changing a climate; spectacular "campaigns"
are substituted for sustained drives toward long-range goals.

The most important service the public broadcasting system
can perform in priorities is to help the American people take
part in the *process* of setting and implementing priorities—in
creating the values and forming the attitudes that make agreement on priorities possible, in comparing and ranking items
according to precedence, in designing the programs of action,
and then in carrying them out. The people should understand,
not just the items chosen for priorities, but the whole context.
They should look ahead to needs and opportunities, not just view
the flames about them.

To further the American people's understanding and to facilitate their participation—these are precisely the major functions the public broadcasting system performs today—with increasing effectiveness for publics that are growing in size and
diversity.

The public broadcasting system can give greater emphasis to
priorities. For example, at their convention in December 1969
the educational broadcasters listed at the top of their programming priorities the problems of environmental destruction and
overpopulation.

These problems illustrate well the need for educational programs that are sustained, varied and deep. The American people have only begun to be dimly aware of these problems. They
have not even begun yet to understand what the complexities
are or what the solutions would require or what the costs would
be. Attempts actually to solve the problems will be divisive.
For example, what smells like pollution to one person may smell
like a job to another. Such problems are here to stay, and the
public broadcasting system can stay with them.[1]

*   *   *

The preservation of the environment and the control of population are only two of many priorities that public broadcasting

can serve. It can serve some priorities through its programming for general audiences. But to serve some other priorities, it must win the cooperation of other institutions and agencies.

For example, the initiative in making the American system of formal education more vital and effective must come from the educational system. But the public broadcasting system can try to act as a "catalytic agent" in removing the blocks to the full use of television and radio.

The field of early childhood education was wide open, and here "Sesame Street" was able to have great impact.

Let us look at some other fields where public broadcasting might be able to render important services.

How can new knowledge about early human growth be translated into parent education? Research indicates that the most important formative period of life is the first few years, even months. Since the publication of Benjamin Bloom's landmark summary,' in centers at Harvard University, the University of Illinois and elsewhere, a great deal has been discovered about early human growth and more is being discovered. Research in other fields reveals that the health and diet of the mother during pregnancy, even before conception, influence foetal development. If the American people really want to provide equal opportunity for all, if they really want to promote the health and well-being of humans, if they want to favor the development of some human characteristics and to discourage the development of others, then they should do something about the period of early human growth, which is the period when the least efforts can produce the greatest results. Yet there has been almost no effort to translate the new knowledge into programs that will help adults, particularly parents and parents-to-be, to apply it.' How can television be used to meet this need?

What is going to be done in the day-care centers that are being established all over the country? In his message on the reform of the welfare program, which linked welfare to work and work to day-care centers, President Nixon said, "This Adminis-

tration is committed to new emphasis on child development in
the first five years of life." But Dr. Jerome Kagan, a member of
the President's Science Advisory Committee on Educational
Research, commented, "Nobody knows what the hell to do with
those little babies once they get into the centers, and we're
going to be in real real trouble." The question now, he said,
is how to make them "minimally malevolent." Can television
be used to make them "minimally malevolent," even maximally
beneficial?

*How can opportunities for basic education be made available
to those adults who want it?* More than 21,000,000 Americans
eighteen years or older have had fewer than seven years of
schooling. Present efforts to meet their needs are grossly inadequate. In an overview of the uses of television for teaching
literacy to adults, Keith Tyler reported: "The advantages of
using instructional television are such that it pays off, both in
terms of quality of instruction and in terms of making use of
volunteer and unqualified classroom teachers, when, say, as few
as fifty groups are involved. Above this arbitrary number, the
economics become increasingly and, finally, overwhelmingly
favorable." [4] Nevertheless, the use of television for teaching
literacy to adults seems to have declined in the United States
since the middle of the 1960's.

At the same time, evidence was accumulating that the problem of illiteracy in the United States is far greater than was
previously recognized—if literacy is defined, as realistically it
must be, in terms of specific reading requirements for specific
people in specific situations. In October 1970 a survey conducted
by Louis Harris and Associates for the new National Reading
Council concluded that 13 percent of the U.S. population over
age sixteen "lacks the reading ability necessary for survival."
Harris said that this figure was conservative and would be 24
percent if the survey had included persons polled who declined
to complete their interviewsw. An even more drastic estimate
was made by David Harman, on leave from the Ministry of
Education and Culture in Israel to work for his doctoral de-

gree at the Harvard Graduate School of Education. "In Adult Basic Education programs in the United States," Harmon pointed out, ". . . the eighth-grade completion equivalency needs to be supplanted by a clearly defined delineation of adult reading requisites and related functional goals. Income tax forms, driving instructions, job application forms, television guides, and newspapers, among others, could be analyzed to derive a precise definition of adult reading level, which could then become the articulated aim of literacy instruction. Functional aspects of the programs should also be clearly delineated and their relationship to literacy defined."

Using "reading requisites and related functional goals" as measurements, Harmon concluded: "United States government figures placing the rate of illiteracy among the population aged fourteen and above at 2.4 percent in 1960 grossly underestimate the extent of the problem. Equally as underestimated is the 8.3 percent figure for functional illiterates in the group aged twenty-five and over. In fact over half of that group may be functionally illiterate." [5]

This—both the decline in the use of television to teach literacy to adults and the more realistic assessment of the size of the task—points up the question, Can television be used more effectively and extensively in basic adult education? [6]

How can opportunities for high-school-equivalency education be expanded for those who want it? About 38,000,000 adults over eighteen years of age have had eight years or more of schooling but have not completed requirements for a high school diploma. One set of examinations—the General Education Development (GED) Test—is now given by all states and territories in the United States, yielding a high-school equivalency certificate to each successful candidate. One video-taped course designed for high school equivalency, "TV High School," produced by J. McFadden, Director, Manpower Education Institute of New York City, has been or is being used by many educational television stations. Several other stations offer courses produced by local schools. However, the number of students enrolled is a small proportion of potential students. A major expansion would require cooperative efforts between the public television system and other agencies. The homogeneous nature of the potential students for high-school-equivalency education and the impressive history of the GED would suggest a large opportunity for the use of television in this priority.

How can community colleges be helped to cope with the tasks that threaten to overwhelm them? They are being established at the rate of one per week. They could be the major ladders of educational opportunity for great numbers of people, both those of college-age and older. Not surprisingly, many of them are unable to perform well either their job as a junior college or their job as a community college. However, the American Association of Junior Colleges is giving strong leadership, and the association has an effective community-service project. How can television be used to multiply and improve the services of this, the fastest growing area in both higher education and the continuing education of adults? [7]

How can education in public affairs be expanded and improved? The quality of the people's understanding and participation determines the quality of their government. Public affairs education occupies a middle ground between highly structured learning, on the one hand, and random learning, on the other. A large body of experience has demonstrated that radio and television broadcasting can be related to groups organized for study and discussion. [8]

Eugene Johnson has written: "Not technology but the integration of educational materials, each with a carefully defined role, is the core of the systems approach. . . . It is difficult to apply the learning system approach to the informal education of large numbers of adults . . . yet, until we learn to do so, this writer remains convinced that we shall not make the massive impact which is essential to any real shift in public attitudes or thinking. Only when the whole of a communty—indeed, the whole of an organized society—is seen as the client and informal educational programs for adults respond to that concept, will education begin to make its full contribution to the shaping of an informed and rational public opinion. Only then will television realize its full potential." [9]

Again, the obstacle of public television's limited air-time emerges; discussion and debate by highly motivated persons should be able to take place when they are home from work, which is also the time when public television has many other tasks to perform for more general audiences. And again, the development of cable television may provide a way to surmount this obstacle.

*   *   *

The brief looks that have been taken above in six fields where public television could render important service to national priority interests all involve special (through large) publics. The limitations of open broadcasting restrict the functions of public broadcasting in these fields; the opening up of more channels through cable television could expand its potentialities. Let us look now at another field that involves *general* audiences and is most appropriate for *open-channel* broadcasting.

The public broadcasting system should given leadership in providing the American people with more open and more free electronic access to the proceedings of their government.

To provide "the American people with electronic access to the proceedings of their government"—what a strange way of putting the issue! It is like saying that the earth revolves around the sun, instead of the sun around the earth; it is like saying that we should feed poor people because they are hungry instead of doing so to get rid of agricultural surpluses. The issue is usually put, *How to let this or that group gain access to television?*

To state the issue in terms of group access to television is to lead into a maze of blind alleys or jungle of complexities, such as those following from the FCC's "fairness doctrine" and "equal-time provision," and from legislative attempts to limit the amount of money that a political candidate may spend for "spot commercials" on television. The fast developing result is a clutter of rules, regulations and laws under which the American people get (or do not get) the portrayal, information, knowledge, analysis, discussion and debate "by the courtesy" or "under the sponsorship" of self-interested government authorities on political grounds rather than through a free press (defined to include the electronic media) on public grounds.

Of course serious problems are involved in the "fairness doctrine," the "equal-time provision" and attempts to make it possible for people without much money to campaign for office. But insofar as these problems are approached with the intent to make more fair or equitable *the access to television,* the fundamental assumption is wrong. For example, the real evil is not that some politicians have more money to spend than others do. The real evil is "selling" candidates as though they are cigarettes or soap or automobiles; it is considering the American people as "purchasers of political products" rather than as self-governing electorates.[10]

The Ptolemaic view (according to which the center of the issue is gaining access to the media) seeks "fairness" and "equality" in the use of the medium, which often means the use of the medium to manipulate people; the quest leads into some blind alleys (such as the achievement of "fair" treatment and "equal" time by granting *no* treatment or *no* time) and some unanswerable questions (such as, Where to end orders for "anti-commercial" commercials? How to distinguish between Presidential utterances made as leader of the nation and those made as leader of his party? Who speaks for Congress? etc.).

The Copernican view (according to which the center of the issue is the people's access through the electronic media to their government) seeks the least filtered view of public proceedings and the richest possible diet of information, background knowledge, analysis, debate and discussion.

Broadcasting, public and private, should be based on the Copernican view. The Federal Communications Act authorizes the FCC to grant licenses to broadcast "in the public interest, convenience or necessity." These words define the obligation that a station undertakes when it accepts a license to broadcast.

The fulfillment of that obligation is the rent he pays for the use of a resource that belongs to the people. That obligation—bearing alike on Congress, the Federal Communications Commission and the stations—has so been defined by the Supreme Court, grounding its decision on the First Amendment to the Constitution. "The public interest, convenience or necessity" has never been, perhaps cannot be, precisely defined, but at least the concept makes the center of the electronic system the public and not the media, and even less the groups who would use the media.

The justification for having a *public* broadcasting system is that the American people need a system whose sole purpose is to serve "the public interest, convenience or necessity" as an alternative to one that has double, and often conflicting, purposes. If broadcasting is to be reoriented to revolve around the basic intent of the First Amendment and the Federal Communications Act, leadership must come from the public broadcasting system.

In the courts, the FCC, Congress, the commercial industry and elsewhere some other people are working for this fundamental reorientation—else the cause would be already lost. But the leadership should properly come from the public broadcasting system.

The consequences of reorientation would lead to many basic changes far beyond broadcasting—the opening up to the electronic media of the sessions and some committee meetings in both houses of Congress; electronic coverage of open sessions of the Federal Communications Commission, the Federal Trade Commission, the Supreme Court, and so on; and, yes, electronic coverage of the open sessions of such "non-governmental governments" as stockholders of large corporations and conventions of labor unions.

If self-government in the United States is to continue and to improve, the issue must be reoriented to center on the people's electronic access to the proceedings of their government. The time is short. The television "image-makers" are increasingly employed. Their skills of "packaging" candidates and issues are

sharpening. The new electronic technology (photography, recording, "bugging," data banks, computer information systems,
etc.) has given governments—official and unofficial—the power
to take note of anything, right or wrong (or both or neither),
relevant or not, that an individual does, says or writes in his
private or public activities. The "information" remains, re-
trievable, duplicable, communicable *forever*—raw, unevaluated,
to be used by faceless people in unknown ways. But the public
does not have even a way of watching and listening to the
public activities of the persons it has elected to Congress.

Referring to this one aspect of a much wider issue, Jack Gould,
television critic of the *New York Times,* has advised:

"Lift the curtain and let's have a real peak into Washington.
If the TV correspondents are rugged gentlemen and fill us in
on why some Congressmen might be especially interested in farm
subsidies, oil depletion allowances or whatever, the relationship
between TV and politics might take some surprising and inviting
twists.

"Thanks to Congress, what the commercial networks do in
the matter of covering members of the Senate and the House is
not absolutely critical. In creating the Corporation for Public
Broadcasting, Congress has committed the taxpayer's dollar
to the support of TV . . . And, since members of Congress already
are the viewers' employes, most of the expense of offering millions the option of an active sense of involvement in government
is currently being paid; the only thing missing is the dividend
in return." [11]

*   *   *

These questions and comments all point to areas where public
broadcasting might be able to serve priorities. Other areas
could be outlined, but the illustrations are perhaps enough to
suggest that rich opportunities lie ahead for public broadcasting,
particularly television, to render services comparable to what it
has already done in early childhood education. Each effort
should follow the process that is now familiar in both education
and broadcasting: the selection of a priority objective, the use
of the systems approach, experimentation and demonstration.

Each effort would require both adequate funding and highly qualified people.

An aspect of the high qualifications that the people in public broadcasting need is the ability to draw upon the talents of people not in broadcasting—for example, in the setting of priorities and in following through on them. Earlier, this chapter noted that the educational broadcasters had listed the problems of environmental destruction and overpopulation at the top of their programming priorities for the 1970's. In so doing, they cannot be given much credit for foresight. Nor can they be blamed much for lack of foresight either, bedeviled as they are by their daily tasks that range from raising money to coaxing inadequate equipment into acceptable performance. The situation indicates the need for public broadcasting to recruit (perhaps as consultants) the thinkers who can foresee events and anticipate issues. The public broadcasting system at all levels should arrange relationships by which the best minds in the country are engaged in a regular way with projecting problems and issues and opportunities. It needs to arrange relationships also with the kinds of people who can help them plan how to transmute anticipated problems, issues and opportunities into systematic, developmental programming. The broadcasters themselves can be presumed to have, or to have access to, the special competencies pertaining to their media, but they need help from experts in many other fields to wed expert insight with expert treatment.

Conclusions

The public broadcasting system is not an end in itself but is a means—among others—to ends that can and should be identified. If the system demonstrates that it can perform valuable service toward the improvement of society, substantial funds may be channeled into it. The most important service it can perform is to improve the people's understanding of their affairs and the quality of their participation.

This line of thought leads to the nature of power and the role of knowledge in the American society.

The basic source of power in a democracy is consensus. Hannah Arendt has written: "Power corresponds to the human ability not just to act, but to act in concert. Power is never the property of an individual. It belong to a group and remains in existence only so long as the group keeps together." However, that statement does not take into account the role of knowledge in the modern society:

"There are many indications that the nature of authority in this century is undergoing profound changes perhaps comparable in magnitude to those that occurred in the Renaissance and Reformation. The change clearly is related to the increasingly important role of knowledge in society. The central social and economic role of land in a feudal society and of machinery in an industrial society is filled by organized knowledge in a science-based, noetic society." [12]

A characteristic of the modern world is the movement toward the application of knowledge organized on a large scale to the achievement of large objectives. The people demand the achievement of large objectives; the interdependence and complexity of modern life require the organization of knowledge on a large scale.

Perhaps the most important consequence of the walks on the moon was that tens of millions of Americans wondered, if we can send men to the moon, why can't we solve problems on Earth?

But there is an essential difference between putting men on the moon and solving the problems on Earth. To put men on the moon, all that the American people were called upon to do was to acquiesce in the expenditure of funds. With enough money, the government could assemble and organize resources, "secure" facilities on Earth and consult only physical conditions in space and on the moon. But on Earth, there is no "Sea of Serenity" or "Sea of Tranquility;" everything, everywhere is the "Ocean of Storms." Besides dealing with "recalcitrant materials," planners are dealing with an order of complexity for which their "models" and analytical tools leave them unprepared. For the successful application of knowledge and skills to the problems of the American society, the people must be active partners at every stage—in understanding the human and personal meanings of what is proposed, in sharing the values that are being advanced, in helping to choose the ends and means, in grasping the essential reasons and facts, and in taking part in the execution of the programs.

There are many gropings in the United States and the world toward a grand design that will enable knowledge organized on a large scale to be applied to large objectives: the spread of the "systems approach," the development of "researches into the future," the establishment of various "think tanks," the attempts to draw up "social indicators," "social accounts," "social models," etc.

On the other hand, many people of many kinds are demanding a "piece of the action," the "right to have a say," a share of the "power."

The problem is one of mediation: How to get those who have the knowledge and power to appreciate that the people must share in the knowledge and the uses of power? How to get the people to appreciate that they themselves need understanding and skills in order to participate effectively for their common good?

To mediate between the sources of knowledge and power, on the one hand, and the people, on the other hand—this is the essential task of the public broadcasting system.

Defining the task in that way gives the context for the key questions: How can the public broadcasting system get funds that are adequate and dependable and at the same time free enough to enable it to make a significant difference in society? How can it work within the political-economic framework of society and still do programming that subjects that framework to searching examination?

This is the crux of the matter. Unless the American people give programming freedom an economic base and insulate it from political pressures, their public broadcasting system will, at

worst, wither away, or at best, become a domestic "Voice of
America"— which would mean the voice of government, whether
the executive branch, the legislative branch or both.

One cannot solve this problem in a book. But one can identify
it as the crux. And one can point to the fact that it has been
solved with some degree of success in Great Britain:

"The BBC is a public service financed by public funds—but
not by direct government grant. Its income comes to the BBC
from the annual license paid by everyone who owns a television
set. The BBC charter, granted periodically by Parliament,
establishes it as a public (but not government controlled) service. Though it is the Government which fixes the license fee
from which the BBC derives its income, governments do not
interfere with the content of the programs. They have been
known, of course, to try (and people do pick up telephones and
talk to other people).

"After less than fifty years' experience the BBC is regarded
(abroad, at least) as one of Britain's finest achievements. Its
political independence and professional standards are envied and
respected as an example to broadcasters in many countries. But
its independence and standards will not be upheld without constant vigilance against political pressures and temptations to win
audiences by lowering standards." [13]

The significance of the British experience lies, not in details
(such as the tax on sets, which has serious shortcomings), but in
the demonstration that *programming can be insulated from
political pressures*. The question is, Will the American people
solve the problem—not for the sake of the public broadcasting
system—but as a means to improve the quality of their lives
and their decision-making?

1. The need for a broadcasting system alternative to the commercial system
that can "stay with" issues because they are important and urgent, rather
than because they are momentarily faddish "concerns," was illustrated by
NBC's cancelling its weekly series on ecology, "In Which We Live." The
program was announced by the network in April along with its plans for

covering the April 22 "Earth Day" observances. It was broadcast first on May 3, 1970, and continued for eight more weeks. Then it was canceled without a public announcement to avoid embarrassment. Reuven Frank, president of NBC News, cited as reason for the cancelation lack of sponsorship and viewer interest, and the tightening of network television budgets.

2. Benjamin S. Bloom, *Stability and Change in Human Characteristics* (New York: John Wiley & Sons, Inc., 1964).

3. A notable exception is *Intellectual Stimulation for Infants and Toddlers,* series material taught to parents of infants age 3 months to 19 months (Gainsville, University of Florida, 1969). This how-to-do-it booklet is especially prepared for parents among the rural poor in the South.

4. I. Keith Tyler, "Combating Illiteracy with Television," *AV Communications Review,* Fall 1965, pp. 309-324.

5. "Illiteracy: An Overview," in *Harvard Educational Review,* A Special Issue: Illiteracy in America, May 1970.

6. In the United States notable efforts to use television in literary instruction to adults have been made by WKNO-TV, Memphis (a pioneering venture), in the Chelsea Closed-Circuit Television Project in New York City and the Operation Alphabet project developed by the Philadelphia Public Schools, which was televised in about a hundred cities. See John Ohliger, *The Mass Media in Adult Education: A Review of Recent Literature* (Syracuse, N.Y.: ERIC Clearing House on Adult Education, November 1968), pp. 58-63, with bibliography. Details about the Memphis project are available from the Laubach Literarcy Fund, P.O. Box 131, Syracuse, New York.

7. In 1969 the Television Consortium of Bay Area Community College was organized to offer televised courses for seven member schools. The intent is "to utilize the resources of the college districts to develop TV programming that would not be possible with the limited resources of any one district." The courses will be broadcast over KGTM-TV, the public television station of the College of San Mateo, California.

8. The most knowledgeable persons in this field are Eugene I. Johnson, Professor of Adult Education, the University of Georgia, Athens; and John Ohliger, Assistant Professor of Adult Education, Ohio State University, Columbus. Johnson organized and managed study-discussion groups using radio in San Bernardino, California, and using television in St. Louis. Ohliger wrote his doctoral dissertation on listening-group projects in more than thirty countries since 1920.

9. Quoted in *The Mass Media in Adult Education: A Review of Recent Literature,* pp. 24-25. The review and its bibliography give many references to the use of broadcasting related to organized study-discussion.

10. For an examination and assessment of the impact of the electronic media on politics, see Edward W. Chester, *Radio, Television and American Politics* (New York: Sheed and Ward, 1969).

11. "The Blooping of the President," *New York Times,* August 23, 1970.

12. James D. Carroll, "Science and the City: The Question of Authority," *Science,* Vol. 163 (February 28, 1969), p. 909.

13. Robin Day, "Troubled Reflections of a TV Journalists," p. 87.

THE PROMETHEAN TASK

The American people are shifting away from values that are basically selfish toward values that give more than lip-service to "the public interest." They are shifting, not because they have "found virtue," but because they are becoming aware that the consquences of unbridled selffishness are intolerable.

Consider shift of values in regard to the technology of electronic communications.

In the late 1920's and early 1930's, Congress turned over to private industry scarce channels for electronic transmission and so hobbled the Federal Communications Commission as to make it little more than a friendly traffic cop for the commercial broadcasting industry.

But gradually certain citizens awakened to the implications of the remark "Let me write a nation's songs and I care not who writes its laws." The real rulers of a society, whether many or few, are those who set the dominant values and priorities. In the United States they are the ones who control commercial broadcasting. They are few and are becoming fewer. They are hidden behind fascinating gadgets. They set public values and priorities, through advertising and entertainment, for their private profit.

Enough citizens awakened to the consequences so that an alternative broadcasting service was started. Contrast the inaction of the 1920's and 1930's to the actions of the 1950's and 1960's. An increasing number of television channels and of FM radio channels was reserved for noncommercial use. Gradually a national system of broadcasting for public purposes is coming into being.

The history of broadcasting in the United States is a part of the larger trend toward concern for the public interest. Let us look at that trend in the most general way.

The Democracy of Large Decisions

Technology is a systematic way of altering the environment. It should, therefore, be regarded as comprising intellectual and institutional tools as well as physical tools. All such tools are here to stay. They give a power, and power will be used. Whether they are good or bad will turn on the purposes they are used for and the way they are used—whether technological advances are reckless of consequences or whether technological change is guided by a deeper concern for the interaction between men's tools and the environment in which they live.

The decision to establish a system of broadcasting for public purposes was a decision to use electronic technology with a keener concern for social consequences. A purpose of the public broadcasting system is to expand the people's decision-making process so that it will have a deeper vision into the interconnectedness of things and a wider moral horizon.

A purpose is to convert the "tyranny of small decisions" into a democracy of large decisions.

A purpose is to promote awareness that there are *no* "external costs" on the spaceship Earth.

A purpose of the public broadcasting system is to help clarify the choices available to the American people and to enlarge the range of choice. Providing a wider range of broadcasting programs is only a means to a wider range of choice in all areas of life, a means of enlarging the range of choice that will be available to people yet unborn.

A purpose of the public broadcasting system is to alert people to the probable consequences of decisions that affect their lives, to act as ombudsman for the hopeless, to act as champion for posterity.

One of its purposes should be to create constituencies, not just for itself, but also for the public interest.

The public broadcasting system should try to improve the *process* of decision-making. It should seek to give context to crisis; to convert anxieties into concerns and discontents into proposals; to change high-decibel talk into high-level discourse;

to translate problems into issues and issues into orderly procedures; to clarify the difference between the urgent and the
important.

The Democracy of Civilization

However, we should not get so caught up in decisions and
processes as to forget that the end of a democratic way of life
is the individual person. In a democracy the quality of any
decision is secondary to the *educational value* of taking part in
the deciding.

Democracy of all kinds is the sharing of action and responsibility for the sake of individual development. Equal opportunities are meaningless without equal responsibility, for it is
responsibility for consequences that induces the most growth.

Democracy of various kinds—political, economic, social—has
been won many times in varying degrees, although never completely. The last kind to be gained, one that has not been
attained to any high degree anywhere, including in the United
States, is what Lyman Bryson called "the democracy of civilization—the full sharing, by right of birth, by every man to the
measure of his native powers in all the values of a national
culture . . ."[1] By "cultural democracy," Bryson meant the full
sharing of such values as beauty, justice, and the search for
truth—above all, the search for truth.

If one were required to list the very first priority for the public broadcasting system, it probably should be the objective of
helping people use the methods of rational inquiry in the search
for truth. This was the method of Prometheus, who, caring for
mankind, looked ahead clearly and dispassionately and was
willing to pay the price he foresaw.

The Triangulation of Truth

In the White House Johnny Cash sang, "Can you blame the
voice of youth for asking, 'What is Truth?'" In the agora of
Athens Socrates was blamed for asking that question. In

Jerusalem Pontius Pilate was not blamed for asking it, because he implied that there is no Truth. Many people today do not even bother to ask the question, either because they believe they already have the Truth or because they believe there are only private truths, which are all created equal.

However, civilization depends upon the acceptance of a common method for determining what is true, or probably true. Each person sees the world differently; everybody can err and lie. These are not new discoveries. But to abandon the ideal of objectivity because it is unattainable is to wash one's hands of responsibility, as Pontius Pilate did. Objective truth is impossible, but a consensus is both possible and necessary. One can try to observe clearly, report honestly, discuss freely and submit to verification.

A public truth is a set of three relationships, with a speaker at one point, a listener at another point and the reality they are observing at a third point. In surveying, triangulation is a technique of establishing an unknown position by using angles or distances from two known positions. The triangulation of truth calls for both doubt of self and respect for others.

The first step in the triangulation of truth is to determine one's own position as accurately as possible and from it to observe the reality as clearly as possible, recognizing that the view is relative to the position.

The second step in the triangulation of truth is to determine the position of the other observer as accurately as possible and to imagine the reality as it must appear from the other point of view, recognizing that it is no more relative than one's own.

The third step in the triangulation of truth is to compare observations of the realty. Reality is known, not "in itself" (whatever that may mean), but only in men's minds. However, there are ways to test how closely images of reality correspond with an objective reality of some kind.

Mankind has paid dearly over the ages for the small degree of freedom he has won to seek truth and the small measure of success he has attained in establishing peaceful methods for the search.

Robert Redfield said:

"Talking is good, and it is necessary to make clear what we truly are. But mutual security depends on mutual understanding, and for understanding you have to have a conversation. A conversation is not two people talking loudly at each other, and certainly is not one person with a megaphone.

"It is first one person listening while the other talks, and then that one talking while the other listens. . . . To engage in conversation is to build the civilization of the dialogue.

"If I should choose a few words to describe the endless set of creation that is education, I should choose these: Education is conversation about the meaning of life, as each sees some part of it, on behalf of everyone."

"Can you blame the voice of youth for asking, 'What is Truth?'" The answer is No. But you can blame any voice, of youth or age, that asks and does not listen when someone tries to answer.

Conversation about the meaning of life, "as each sees some part of it, on behalf of everyone," must widen as people become more interdependent. It must deepen as Man's power and responsibility increase. He now has such power that he is responsible for the future of himself, of Earth and perhaps beyond. He has evolved into the chief agent of the evolution of of all forms of life on Earth—perhaps the only place in the universe where life is.

No machine, no methodology, no system can get Man off the hook of responsibility. Man is conscious only in the individual human being who is each and all of us.

Therefore, Man's responsibility is the individual person's responsibility. That ancient personal prescripton may seem to be weak medicine—superstitional, pre-scientific—amid the social pharmacopoeia of wonder-drug projects and large-scale programs, but ultimately it is all we have. The ingredients of this homely prescription are the simples of honesty, modesty and compassion. Each of us needs to receive and give all the help he can.

The public broadcasting system is engaged in the Promethean task of helping people learn by feeling compassionately and by thinking clearly and dispassionately.

Those words may sound "unrealistic" amid the crumbling of consensus and the clash of violence. But there are two reasons why we can hope.

One reason is Man's capacity to learn. Having got into an impasse through learning to do so much, he may now learn enough to get out of it.

The other reason why we can hope is that we do not know the future. Prometheus brought man the gift of fire, the basis for technology. He brought another gift also:

Chorus: Did you perhaps go further than you have told us?

Prometheus: I caused mortals to cease foreseeing doom.

Chorus: What cure did you provide against that sickness?

Promotheus: I placed in them blind hopes.

We can hope—and work to realize our hopes. The sin against hope is the ultimate sin. Our hope may be blind, but our work to fulfill our hope must be clear- and far-sighted.

Our work must be, first, to establish a financial base for public broadcasting that is strong, assured, and insulated from political pressure. Until such base is built, the hopes of the American people for a medium that is *their instrument* will remain like Tantalus' hopes for food and drink—so near, and yet so far.

1. Lyman Bryson, *The New Prometheus* (New York: Macmillan Company, 1941).

DATE DUE

10. 22. '81	
5. 26. '83	
10. 04. '84	
2. 21. '85	
2. 21. '85	
10. 02. '85	
11. 27. '85	

Robert J./The people's instrume

3 5209 00414 7514